The Church In Many Houses

The Church In Many Houses

Reaching Your Community through Cell-Based Ministry

Steve Cordle

Abingdon Press
Nashville

The Convergence eBook Series

The Church in Many Houses:
Reaching Your Community through Cell-Based Ministry

Edited by Tom Bandy and Bill Easum
Copyright © 2005 by Steve Cordle

This book is printed on acid-free, recycled, elemental-chlorine-free paper.

Library of Congress Cataloging-in-Publication Data

Cordle, Steve.

The church in many houses : reaching your community through cell-based ministry / Steve Cordle.

p. cm. -- (The convergence ebook series)

Includes bibliographical references (p.   ).

ISBN 0-687-32579-X (alk. paper)

1. Small groups--Religious aspects--Christianity. 2. Church development, New. 3. Church growth. I. Title. II. Series: Convergence series.

BV652.2.C668 2005

253'.7--dc22

2004027708

05 06 07 08 09 10 11 12 13 14—10 9 8 7 6 5 4 3 2 1

MANUFACTURED IN THE UNITED STATES OF AMERICA

TO LINDA
The wife of my youth

Contents

Foreword

By Mike Slaughter, pastor of Ginghamsburg Church and author of *UnLearning Church.*

I have experienced more change in the first years of this new millennium than the first three decades of my ministry combined. The strategies we trusted to draw baby boomers to church in the '80s and '90s are not working with the under-forty crowd. The complexity of the mega-mall ministry structure that became a phenomenon in the '90s has not proven to be reproducible for the vast majority of Christian leaders.

Transformational twenty-first-century churches are rediscovering the DNA that made the Church radical and effective in its earlier years. Three emerging trends distinguish these churches from their baby boomer counterparts of the last decade.

Back to Basics

The emerging church is working from a simple strategy: Pare down the complex programs and concentrate on the basics. These churches are not trying to be all things to all people by having great men's ministries, women's ministries, singles' ministries, recreation ministries, etc. It is the simple strategy of bringing people into a life relationship with Jesus, who will grow in vital discipleship in the context of cell community, and then serve the mission of Christ through their call and giftedness.

Bigger Isn't Better

Many of us in the mega-church movement unintentionally began to see size as the measure of strength. Size is not a strategy for discipleship. The emerging church understands that strength is not measured by how "fat" you are, but by how "fit" you are. The question that needs to be asked is how many people are serving the mission of Jesus—not how many are attending. After all, Jesus had a church that only numbered one hundred and twenty by the end of his earthly ministry. The strategy: Build true disciples—not numbers.

Relationship Centered

My generation built churches that were centered on great worship. We

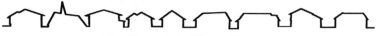

majored in worship arts and mastered digital worship. "Build powerful worship and they will come" was our mantra. However, twenty-first century churches are creating authentic community.

Steve Cordle has captured the heart behind the success of the New Testament Church that spread rapidly throughout the Roman world in less than a century. The key: Simple organisms grow faster than complex ones. The life of the body is in the *cell*.

Preface

By Joel Comiskey, author of *Home Cell Group Explosion*, and *How to Be a Great Cell Group Coach*.

The cell church movement is a worldwide phenomenon and the largest churches in the world are cell-based. Many U.S. pastors, noting the growth of these worldwide churches, have tried copying their models, hoping for similar success. Most have failed.

Dr. Steve Cordle pinpoints how to avoid similar failures. Steve is certainly qualified to write this book. Steve wrote his doctoral dissertation on small group ministry and understands the concepts very well. Yet, Steve went beyond theory and in 1991 planted a church from scratch that has now grown to over one thousand in Sunday attendance. Steve has increasingly focused his church down the cell church path because he understands that it's the best way to produce disciples who are producing disciples.

Certainly Steve's church, Crossroads United Methodist Church, has experienced its share of false starts and mid-course corrections in its cell church journey. Yet, I'm excited to say that Crossroads UMC is now one of the leading, cutting-edge cell models in the U.S. today. Crossroads UMC exemplifies to others that cell church ministry is a viable option in the U.S. and works in North America just as it does overseas. There are essential principles, however, to making cell church work in North America. This book explains those principles.

I recommend this book so highly because of its balance. Pastor Steve draws on solid research from worldwide cell churches, church history (especially John Wesley's small group revival), and provides practical keys for those wanting to make cell church work in North America.

This is a must-read book for those interested in making disciples who make disciples through the local church in North America and beyond.

Acknowledgements

Many thanks to:

- The staff, coaches, and leaders of Crossroads Church who, live out the vision with faith and determination.

- Joel Comiskey, whose patient tutoring has taught me so much about the cell church. Without his influence, Crossroads would not be a cell-based church today.

- Linda, my wife, my cheerleader; and my children Josh (and Christina!) and Jonathan and Daniel, who put up with my typing at odd places and times.

- Mark Belko for assistance in reading and editing the manuscript.

- Karen Bushnell for proofreading and feedback.

- Bill Easum, for the encouragement to put these thoughts into writing.

Introduction

It was very early in the morning, and I sat in our church's prayer room, my mind racing. I had just finished reading a book called *Home Cell Group Explosion*, by Joel Comiskey. True to its title, the book's message detonated inside me like a bomb. It described how churches around the world were reaching and discipling huge numbers of people through multiplying networks of cell groups.

To add to its impact, days earlier I had returned from a trip to Korea, where I had seen God's power at work in two of the world's largest churches. It turns out they were both cell-based congregations. Cell ministry had my attention.

As I sat in the prayer room that morning, the question careening through my mind was: "Could it work here?" Was cell ministry effective only in Asia or Central America, or would it work in Oakdale, Pennsylvania, too?

I had planted Crossroads United Methodist Church seven years before. Like many new churches, we had been helped greatly and influenced by both Willow Creek and Saddleback Churches. We developed a seeker-sensitive worship style, and built small groups right into the foundation of the church (using the "meta-church" philosophy). We were growing numerically, and in most respects we were a thriving congregation.

Yet amidst the many positive vital signs, I knew that our small group ministry was losing steam. Our coaches told me the groups were becoming stale. They were not multiplying, and the leaders were feeling tired. If small groups were to become the base of our church, that needed to change.

After my visit to Korea and reading Comiskey's book, our staff began discussing whether Crossroads should adopt the cell-based approach. We read and we learned all that we could about cell ministry. We prayed and discussed the issue from all angles. I'm sure the staff grew tired of all the deliberating and longed for a decision. But I was hesitant. I didn't know everything about the cell church, but it was obvious to me that changing to the cell model would affect more than our small group approach. To become a cell-based church would fundamentally change the way we did ministry. To add to my uncertainty, I didn't know of many thriving cell-based churches in the United States. Nonetheless, my attraction to what I knew of the cell model continued to increase.

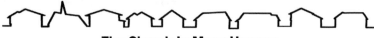

"What kind of church do you want?"

Finally, we decided to take the plunge and pursue a cell strategy. I wish I could say the rest of the story was one of steady growth, enthusiasm, and success. It didn't work out exactly that way.

We experienced a mixture of success and frustration. We saw many lives change, and other people resist and object. We adopted some parts of the cell strategy, but were unaware or not ready to adopt other pieces. At one point we pulled back, reorganized, and then started again.

At times I had serious doubts as to whether cell church ministry would work here. In some ways it would have been easier to do ministry in a form that is more in line with people's expectations.

But something inside of me wouldn't let me let go of the dream. I can't say I caught the vision of the cell church; rather, the cell church vision caught me. I couldn't shake it. I was driven to pursue the cell-based ministry not because of the size of church it can grow, but because of the quality of disciple it can develop. In my visits to thriving cell churches I met numerous church members and cell leaders who demonstrated the character of Christ in ways I had rarely seen. When asked, they could readily articulate their church's vision. More than that, reaching and discipling unreached people was regarded as a normal activity, and most members knew how to do it (or at least how to learn to do so).

I asked myself: "What kind of church do I want to invest my life in building?" I knew I didn't want to settle for simply persuading people to attend services, give, and behave. I yearned for a church that could become a Kingdom movement like I read about in the book of Acts. I longed to see unreached people deeply transformed into the image of Jesus. I saw so much potential for authentic New Testament life in the cell approach that I was determined to figure out how it could work in our setting.

Today, Crossroads has made the transition and become a cell-based church, and it has been well worth the journey! Yes, there is more work to be done before all our members fully understand and own cell church principles, but the cell mindset has taken hold. Many lives are being changed and healed at wonderfully deep levels. People who never thought they could minister to others are now leading cell groups. We are still a "work in progress," but we are making disciples who make disciples.

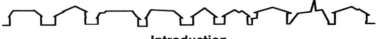

Discovering the Principles

This book is not about Crossroads Church, though; it is about the unique principles that shape the cell church, and how they differ from the assumptions of traditional, program-based churches. The process of becoming a cell church is more about embracing cell philosophy than adopting certain methods. There are many excellent books that describe the "how" and the "what" of cell ministry. This is an attempt to answer the question, "Why?"

The first section of the book will acquaint you with the basics of the cell church model. Chapter one provides an overview of the worldwide cell church movement. Chapter two introduces the distinctive cell church disciple-making strategy. In chapter three, we see that the cell church model corresponds closely with both Jesus' disciple-making strategy and with the ministry components of Wesley's early Methodist movement.

Part Two is the core of the book. It describes the fundamental shifts in thinking that are required for the cell church strategy to work.

The final section addresses some practical and spiritual aspects of cell-based ministry.

This book does not advocate a specific cell model, because methods are always changing. It is about essential principles that can be applied in many different ways depending on the context. In fact, I am sure that by the time this book reaches your hands we will have modified some of the methods I have referred to as we learn more effective ways of doing ministry. However, those changes will be guided by the principles you will read here.

As you read about the cell church in these pages, I want to be clear that there is no such thing as "the" cell church method. There are a variety of practices used by those who would call themselves cell churches. I will often refer to the way we do cell ministry at Crossroads, but other cell churches might use different methods.

For clarity, I am going to use the term "cell" when referring to groups, even though not all churches use that word. At Crossroads we currently use the term "small group." Other churches use different names, like Life Group, home group, etc.

God is always renewing and directing the Church. In the pages to follow you will read about some fresh ways God is at work through the emerging cell church movement.

Part I
The Emerging Cell Church Movement

CHAPTER ONE

Signs of Hope

On November 23, 2002, 150,000 people gathered in a large open air meeting space in San Salvador, El Salvador.[1] The crowd was not assembled for a sporting event or a rock concert; it had come to worship. Amazingly, almost all those gathered belonged to one church: La Mision Cristiana Elim (Elim Church).

A church that is the size of a small city is bound to attract attention, and Elim has done just that, both in Latin America and beyond. Yet, Elim has not always been a huge church attracting international visitors. In the late 1970s the church consisted of only a few hundred people. Elim's incredible growth started after founding Pastor Sergio Solorzazo was sent to Seoul, Korea in order to learn about a ministry philosophy called "cell-based" ministry. Since adopting the cell approach in 1986, Elim has grown at a truly remarkable pace. Today, there is not a building large enough for the whole congregation to meet, so from time to time the church rents sports stadiums for worship.[2] Tens of thousands of lives have been transformed by the power of Christ through Elim Church's ministry.

The church that inspired Elim is Yoido Full Gospel Church in Seoul, Korea. It is the largest church in the world, reporting well over seven hundred thousand members. Yoido is not only a cell-based church, it also known as the birthplace of the modern cell church movement. Yoido became a cell-based ministry out of necessity. Pastor David Cho had planted the church in 1961 and seen it grow to over two thousand people under his leadership. However, in trying to keep up with the demands of the growing congregation single-handedly, Cho worked so hard that he suffered a serious physical and emotional collapse in 1964. He was unable to resume full-time pastoral duties for ten years. During his time of forced rest, Cho searched for a way to keep the church's ministry growing. He felt led by God to designate lay leaders and to give them pastoral authority over a small group of other members. These leaders not only facilitated weekly group meetings, they also fulfilled pastoral care functions and led the members in reaching out to others in evangelism.

The resulting growth was truly explosive. When Cho was finally able to resume his ministry on a full-time basis, the church was many times larger than when he left it. By 1980 the church had one hundred thousand members and was the largest in the world. At one point in the 1980s Yoido was seeing up to twelve thousand people *per month* convert from Buddhism, secularism, and nominal faith.[3] Yoido's remarkable ministry has influenced churches all around the world, prompting many to become cell-based congregations.

Now, at the dawn of the twenty-first century, the cell-based philosophy of ministry has taken root in all parts of the globe. Today, nineteen of the twenty largest churches in the world are cell churches.[4] In addition to Elim and Yoido churches, a few of the notable cell-based ministries include:

- International Charismatic Mission in Bogotá, Columbia; more than forty-five thousand in worship attendance.

- Kensington Temple, London, England; attendance of more than ten thousand.

- Works and Mission Baptist Church, Ivory Coast, Africa; attendance with satellite sites: 150,000.

- Bethany World Prayer Center, Baton Rouge, Louisiana: More than ten thousand attendance.

Signs of Hope

These and other huge cell-based churches are noteworthy for more than their impressive statistics. These churches represent hope. In a world wracked with monumental crises such as war, starvation, AIDS, family disintegration, and loss of personal meaning, it is easy to become resigned to the broken state of humanity. But the effectiveness of these dynamic cell churches demonstrates that a local church can significantly penetrate a region with the light of the gospel.

The root of the world's problems can be found in the human heart. People starve because other people allow them do so. There can be no peace between nations without people who love peace. Families only stay healthy when the family members exhibit love and faithfulness. In order for the world to change, individual hearts must be changed by the power of God.

When people are changed from grasping to giving, from lustful to loving, from rage-filled to blessing others, then the social system in which they live will change also. Transformed lives can result in changed families, which can result in changed communities, and, at least in part, a changed world. In short, the kingdom of God breaks in. God has chosen to make the Church the instrument through which God will extend the kingdom. When the Church reaches the unreached by demonstrating and proclaiming the gospel, God's kingdom advances.[5]

Most local churches desire to be agents of God in spreading the Good News. They want see God's kingdom come. However, research shows us that most churches have not been as effective as they would like to be in reaching our needy world. In spite of an increasing number of mega-churches, worship attendance in America is not growing. Three out of four churches in the United States are plateaued or declining in attendance. Roughly half the churches in the United States did not add a single person by confession of faith in the past year. Nearly three times as many churches in America are closing (3,750) as are opening (1,300) each year.[6] Veteran church researcher George Barna concludes, "Despite the activity and chutzpah emanating from thousands of congregations, the Church in America is losing influence and adherents faster than any other major religious institution in the nation."[7] Many have been concerned that even where the church has increased in numbers, the church has been "a mile wide and an inch deep." After surveying and analyzing the beliefs and practices of both Christians and non-Christians in America, Barna finds, "Most Christians . . . think and behave no differently from anyone else."[8]

Clearly, the church needs to discover more effective ways of accomplishing its God-given mission. That is why the growth of these cell churches is so encouraging. They have demonstrated that it is possible to lead large numbers of unreached people into a life-transforming relationship with Jesus Christ.

The vast majority of cell churches will never become as huge as the ones mentioned earlier. However, the fact that some cell churches have grown to such incredible sizes indicates that their ministry approach can be very effective at making disciples. The ministry principles that allowed these flagship churches to grow so large can also be used by new and modest-sized churches, enabling them to reach their own neighborhoods with the gospel.

Quality and Quantity

Cell churches have shown the ability not only to reach large numbers of converts, but also to disciple them to be fully-devoted followers of Jesus.

I saw this in a vivid way one hot August night in Korea in 1998. I was part of a group of pastors visiting Kwang Lim Methodist Church. With 85,000 members, Kwang Lim is the largest Methodist church in the world. As part of our visit, we were taken to Kwang Lim's Prayer Mountain, a retreat center dedicated solely to prayer. Even though we arrived in the middle of the week, we found hundreds of believers gathered in the chapel for an all-night prayer event. After touring the rest of the facility we were escorted to our rooms for the night. As I drifted off to sleep, I could hear through my window the sounds of the leaders reading the Bible and praying. When I awoke for a 5:00 a.m. Communion service, I could still hear the voices of the leaders in passionate prayer (though they were somewhat hoarse by this time). Our group of American pastors and I left humbled by their commitment to prayer, fasting, and the cause of Christ. As we experienced these believers' generosity, attitude of service, and commitment to the gospel, we realized that Kwang Lim Church may be huge, but it is also deep.

It is not unusual for visitors of cell churches all around the world to attest to the vitality and dedication seen in the lives of the members. Cell-based ministry is proving to be remarkably effective at making more *and* better disciples of Jesus Christ.

What is a cell-based church?

Noted cell church researcher Joel Comiskey offers this simple and clear definition of a cell church: "a church that has placed evangelistic small groups at the core of its ministry". [9] The word "evangelistic" is crucial to this definition. In a cell-based church, small groups are outward oriented. The group's mission centers on reaching pre-Christians, not only on caring for believers. Some program-based churches divide their congregation into small groups in order to care for them better. However, in a cell church people are both reached and discipled through cell groups right from the start.

Putting cell groups at the core of the church's ministry means that the leaders and the structures of the church are focused on launching, equipping, multiplying, and nurturing healthy cell groups. In a cell church there is an equal emphasis on the large gathering (worship service/celebration) and the small group (the cell). It has been said that cell and celebration are the two wings of the cell church.[10] They are both equally necessary if the church is going to soar.

A cell church is not defined by size, worship style, socioeconomic group, or geographic location. Neither is a cell church simply a church with small groups. In recent decades many North American churches have discovered that small groups can be effective means of providing relationships, pastoral care, and Bible study. Church members are encouraged to become part of a small group in order to grow spiritually and receive pastoral care. Many believers have benefited greatly from this kind of small group ministry. But the cell church is not just a church with small groups. Cell groups are not just another program of the cell church—they are the basic unit and expression of the church. The most basic difference between cell churches and non-cell churches is the definition of a cell group.

What is a cell group?

The word "cell" is a biological term. The human body is composed of millions of cells, each of which contains the DNA of the body and multiplies itself many times. Similarly, the cell group is the basic unit of life in the body of Christ. The "DNA" of the church is contained in the cell group. That is, the purposes of the church are carried out in the cell.

In some ministry philosophies, almost any gathering that is small and that is related to the church is called a small group (or even a cell group). Using this approach, churches have started motorcycle small groups, Bible study small groups, parking lot volunteer small groups, marriage small groups, and so on. These groups can benefit believers in many ways, but they are probably not cell groups.

Joel Comiskey provides us with an incisive definition: A cell group is "a group of three to fifteen people that meets weekly outside the church building for the purpose of evangelism, community, and discipleship with the goal of multiplication."[11] This definition points out that cell groups, like other small groups, do help Christians grow spiritually. In addition, the regular contact with a few other believers provides a setting conducive to the members establishing warm relational bonds with each other.

However, cell groups do more than foster fellowship and learning. One way cell groups differ from other small groups is that they are fundamentally outward focused. The group's goal is to reach unreached people and lead them into a relationship with Jesus Christ. In the process the group will grow spiritually and multiply numerically. Indeed, if the group does not multiply, it has not fulfilled its purpose. (We will see why this is so in chapter six.)

Of course, each newly formed group requires a new leader. Where are these leaders found? In the cell group! Healthy cell groups produce new

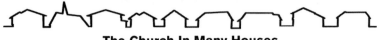
leaders. The cell church itself can be described as a leadership-development engine. The goal of the cell-based church is to help equip Christians for the ministry of making disciples who make disciples.

More Than a Fad

Although the cell-based church is gaining visibility and popularity today, it is not really a new approach. Cell ministry has its roots in the New Testament and in church history. The first Christians met in both large gatherings (in the temple) and in small groups (in homes).[12] We can see the early church's rhythm of "cell and celebration" in these passages from the book of Acts:

> Every day they continued to meet together in the temple courts. They broke bread in their homes and ate together with glad and sincere hearts (Acts 2:46 NIV).

> Day after day, in the temple courts and from house to house, they never stopped teaching and proclaiming the good news that Jesus is the Christ (Acts 5:42 NIV).

Although the church eventually moved away from this dual emphasis, cell ministry has repeatedly reappeared throughout church history. In eighteenth-century England, the Methodist Church was actually born as a cell church. John Wesley adapted the model of cell and celebration to his time. His ministry grew and endured because of the small group system he established.

The spiritual needs of today's world are undeniably great. Could the cell ministry philosophy be a way to meet the deep spiritual needs of our communities? Could it be a way to reach a generation that has been shaped more by popular culture than by a biblical worldview?

The cell church model worked for Wesley, and it has scriptural precedence. It produces dynamic churches in Latin America, Asia, and Africa. But the question is, can the cell approach work in twenty-first-century North America? Or is it effective only in certain cultures?

Before examining that question, let's get a clearer idea of just how cell-based churches operate, and what it is like to be a part of one. In the next chapter we will learn about the cell-based church's distinctive disciple-making strategy as we follow the story of one person's growth from first-time guest to leader of leaders.

NOTES

1. Data from personal e-mail from Joel Comiskey.

2. From David Cho Evangelistic Mission website:
   http://www.davidcho.com/NewEng/cc-2-3.asp

3. Paul Y. Cho, *Prayer: Key to Revival* (Waco, TX: Word Publishing, 1984), 9.

4. Ralph Neighbor, Jr., *Where Do We Go From Here?* (Houston, TX: Touch Publications, 2000), 37.

5. This is not to deny the importance of structural and institutional changes in society. Those are necessary too, but they will be best initiated and sustained by individuals who are being transformed by the grace of Christ.

6. Tom Clegg, Lost in America (Loveland, CO: Group Publishing, 2001), 25-30.

7. George Barna, *The Second Coming of the Church* (Nashville, TN: Word Publishing, 1998), 1.

8. Ibid., 7.

9. William Beckham, *The Second Reformation* (Houston, TX: Touch Publications, 1995).

10. Joel Comiskey, *Home Cell Group Explosion* (Houston, TX: Touch Publications, 1998), 17.

11. Joel Comiskey, *Cell Church Solutions* (Moreno Valley, CA: CCS Publishing, 2005), 12.

12. For more on this, see *The Second Reformation* by William Beckham, *20/20 Vision* by Dale Galloway, and *Reap the Harvest* by Joel Comiskey.

CHAPTER TWO

What Happened When Martha Went to Church

"So if anyone is in Christ, there is a new creation: everything old
has passed away; see, everything has become new!"
—*2 Corinthians 5:17, NRSV*

As I walked down the steps to my home office on my first day as a new
church planter, the reality of my task sank in. I was now officially the pastor of a church that had no members, no building, no land, and no visibility in the community. I had to figure out how to reach unreached people or I wouldn't be there long!

Statistics told me there were many people living in our region who did not
usually attend weekend worship services. They were surely good citizens and
likeable neighbors, but church was simply not a part of their lives. Their Sunday morning routine was comprised of activities such as sleeping late, reading the newspaper, and doing household projects. What would prompt
unchurched people to start setting their alarm clocks and driving to a local
restaurant banquet room to worship God? What could I do to alter their
established patterns?

To make the challenge even more difficult, my real mission went far beyond
changing people's Sunday morning routines. I was praying that Jesus Christ
would become the center of their lives. In other words, my goal was for
unreached people to change their values, priorities, and what they believed
to be true about life. The goal was for them to display faith in a God they
had never seen, and base their lives on a two-thousand-year-old mission.

Motivating an unchurched person to begin regularly attending worship is
difficult enough, but to truly change the core of a person's life requires
nothing less than a miracle of God. Yet this is precisely the challenge faced
by every local congregation, whether it is new or established. The mission
of each church is to reach unreached people and to lead them to become
disciples of Jesus.

What practical steps can a local church take to facilitate this mission?
Obviously, it is the power of God that changes lives. Nothing we do

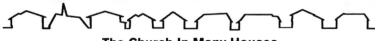

actually transforms someone's inner being or spiritual reality. But God does call the church to play a crucial role in the disciple-making process. Our actions make a difference.

Cell-based churches employ a distinctive and deliberate disciple-making strategy. The following true story illustrates how unreached people can grow into disciples who make disciples through a cell-based ministry. Terms that are highlighted with bold type are key components of Crossroads Church's ministry, and will be explained later in the chapter.

It was the end of the school day, and Mike was on his way out of the building when he overheard Martha, a fellow music teacher, crying in her classroom. Mike paused, then ventured into the room to ask her what was wrong. Martha was slightly embarrassed to be discovered, but since she and Mike were friends, she shared what was going on. Her marriage of ten years was ending in a difficult divorce, and she was crying because she had just opened her first paycheck as a single mother. Not only was she going to have a hard time meeting basic expenses, but also Christmas was approaching and she did not have money to buy gifts for her three young sons. The realization had hit her hard.

Mike listened empathetically and did his best to encourage her. He knew that he could not solve all of Martha's problems himself, but in the days that followed Mike did his best to help. He contributed some of his family's Christmas money to help buy gifts for her children. He also prayed for Martha. Since Mike was a member of one of Crossroads Church's cell groups, it was natural for him to ask his fellow members to pray for her, too. In the weeks that followed, his group prayed that Martha would experience God's love in a personal way.

In the past, Martha had always politely declined Mike's invitations to attend a worship service at Crossroads Church. But now, facing a personal crisis and having received kindness from Mike, she decided to take him up on his offer.

When Martha attended her first service she was surprised at what she found. From the moment she walked in the door people welcomed her with genuine warmth. She had expected the worship service to be dry and boring. It wasn't. Both the music and message spoke to her deeply, and during the service Martha's battered spirit was overwhelmed with a sense of hope and peace. She was anxious to return again the following week. Soon she was attending regularly.

What Happened When Martha Went to Church

Martha was starting to feel close to God in a way that she had not experienced before. Life still was not easy, but she felt the assurance that she was not alone. She wanted to keep growing in her newly awakened faith.

The longer Martha attended Crossroads Church, the more she heard about cell groups. Of course, she knew Mike was in a cell group, and when she attended the Newcomers Class, groups were featured prominently. She also noticed that the pastor referred to groups in many of his sermons.

However, Martha had never been part of a cell group before, and she was uneasy about the idea of going to someone's home to talk about spiritual things. She felt unqualified to talk about the Bible, and she didn't want to appear stupid. Nonetheless, in a moment of courage, she decided to take the plunge. When a cell leader named Teresa invited her to a group meeting, Martha agreed.

As the day for the group meeting approached, Martha started to second-guess her decision to attend. She was nervous about what might happen in a group, and she reasoned that she had a hard enough time juggling life as a working single mom without adding the obligation of a weekly night out. But Teresa was lovingly persistent. She continued to invite Martha, finally suggesting, "Come two times, and if you don't like it, I'll never bug you again." So Martha decided to give it a try.

The first night Martha attended the group, the love and support that flowed from the members enveloped her. Toward the end of the meeting the members held hands and prayed for one another. Martha said, "I cried throughout the whole prayer. It was just what I needed!" She became a regular part of the group.

Now Martha found herself actually looking forward to two church gatherings per week: the worship celebration and her group meeting. The celebration services were inspirational and encouraging. The cell group helped her understand how to apply the Bible to her daily life. She also loved the way the members shared their lives with each other and reached out to non-members.

As she progressed along her spiritual journey, Martha was amazed and encouraged by the way her prayers were being answered. Whenever she had a need, she asked for God's help. Bags of groceries would appear on her doorstep, and anonymous gifts arrived at just the right time. She frequently saw God's power at work in her life.

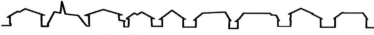

As time went on, more new people responded to invitations to join the group, and Martha's cell grew larger. Teresa, the group leader, had always reminded the members that the purpose of their group was to multiply into two groups. Martha noticed that lately Teresa had been sharing the leadership of the group with another member named Barb. As an apprentice, Barb would become a group leader once the group multiplied.

Eventually, Teresa announced she was leaving to start a new group. Martha was a little sad at the news, but she knew it was vital that the group multiply if it was going to fulfill its mission. Plus, knowing the members would continue to be friends outside of the group comforted Martha. Some members chose to go with Teresa to start a new group, while others remained as a group under Barb's leadership. Martha decided to be part of Barb's cell.

Martha continued to grow in her faith. Her spiritual journey moved to another level when, at Barb's suggestion, she attended a church-sponsored weekend called Encounter Retreat. The Encounter was one of the most meaningful weekends of Martha's life. During those twenty-eight hours, she experienced the love and grace of Christ in a very personal and powerful way. She later reflected, "It was the first time that the forgiveness of God really sunk in." Martha left the Encounter feeling spiritually energized, free, and victorious. She was all the more determined to help others find what she had.

Barb could see that Martha's faith was growing and that she had an open, teachable attitude. One day Barb pulled Martha aside and asked her to consider becoming her apprentice. Barb explained that as an apprentice Martha would share group leadership so that she could become a group leader herself. She assured Martha that she didn't need to know anything about how to lead a group yet. She would receive both on-the-job training (from Barb in the group), and classroom instruction at the church's School of Discipleship. After some thought and prayer, Martha agreed. She enrolled in the School of Discipleship and started to learn more about the faith and about group leadership.

Meanwhile, the members of Barb's group were inviting others to join, and the group was growing larger. No one was surprised when one night Barb announced that she would be leaving to start a new group, and that Martha would take over as leader of the remaining group.

Martha was a little nervous about serving as a leader, but she was reassured that she was not going to be left on her own. Barb explained that

now that the group had multiplied, she would act as Martha's coach. So Martha led her own group weekly, and then met regularly with Barb in a coaching group. They discussed group issues, but they also talked about life in general. After all, they were friends! Martha appreciated knowing someone was praying for her. Anytime she had questions or concerns about what to do as a leader, she would call Barb for guidance.

Martha's group was going well. She was replicating what she had seen in the ministries of Teresa and Barb. The group grew in number, and Martha realized she would need an apprentice so that her group could multiply. She approached a group member named Rick, and he agreed to share the leadership with her and start the process of becoming a leader himself.

Not long afterward, Martha met some women in the community who were going through some difficult times. They were struggling with health issues, marriage difficulties, and generally needed God's love. Martha started to feel the tug on her heart to reach out to these women. After all, they were not part of any church, and they were facing their challenges alone. Moreover, they all lived near Martha.

Martha knew what God was prompting her to do. She turned her group over to her apprentice, Rick. He had also been through the Encounter and the School of Discipleship, and he was more than ready to step up to leadership himself.

As Martha started her new group, she realized that she was now ministering to women who were in a position similar to the one she was in just a few years before!

Martha has been healed, and her life restored by the grace and power of God. Her young children asked to be baptized, and they pray together as a family. Martha is not only leading a cell group, she is also coaching another group leader.

Reflecting on how she has changed, Martha said, "Before I came to Crossroads I would say I believed in God, but I was depressed and fearful about the future. Now I know no matter what happens I have a God who loves me, and who is with me every step of the way. That is peace and absolute joy! I now have an eternal perspective. God has given me a desire to reach out to others, and made it easy for me to talk about God with other people."

At a recent group-leader retreat, Martha casually introduced herself to another leader. Recognizing Martha's name, the other leader exclaimed,

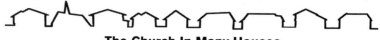

"Oh, so you're the one we were praying for a few years ago in our group!" Tears welled up in Martha's eyes, tears of gratitude and amazement over what God had done in her life, and for the people who made it possible.

Understanding the Cell-based Ministry Strategy

People do not become mature disciples overnight. Spiritual growth happens through a process, and the cell-based ministry strategy is designed to facilitate that process.

At Crossroads, we describe the process of disciple-making in terms of four basic steps: 1) reach, 2) connect, 3) equip, and 4) send. Many program-based churches could also subscribe to these four steps, even if they use different terms. What makes the cell-based approach unique is the definition of words like "equip" and "send," and the ways in which cell churches carry out these steps.

A CELL-BASED
DISCIPLE MAKINGSTRATEGY

1. REACH

Worship Celebration

Cell group

2. CONNECT

Newcomers Class

Encounter Retreat

3. EQUIP

School of Discipleship

4. SEND

Coaching Groups

While not everyone takes these steps in precisely the same order, each element is essential. Many of the steps I describe below are also discussed elsewhere in the book.

Step 1: REACH

Whether we use the term seekers, unchurched, pre-Christians, or something else, if a church is going to fulfill its purpose, it must reach people who are not actively following Christ and help them start doing so. The primary (though not exclusive) ways a cell church reaches people is through the personal faith sharing of cell group members, and through inviting people to its corporate worship services (celebrations) and to its small groups (cells). It is not important whether people first attend a worship celebration and then become involved in a cell group, or vice versa. The goal is that eventually everyone will participate in both.

Though Martha did not realize it, a cell group was responsible for her connection with Crossroads Church. It was a cell group that helped Mike grow in his faith to the point where he wanted to reach out to others. So when Mike learned of Martha's need, he was ready to pray for her and invite her to the worship celebration.

Both the cell and celebration are essential to the cell-based church. They are the two "wings" of the church. To ask which one is more important is like asking a pilot which wing of the airplane is most important; when you are in the air both of them are vital! Let's take a look at both of the church's wings.

The Cell Group

A cell group is more than a Bible study group, and it is more than a meeting. At its essence, a cell group is a set of Christ-centered relationships that is focused primarily on evangelism and discipleship. It is the basic expression of the church, because the essential purposes of the church are fulfilled through the cell. In a healthy cell group, members do not limit their contact with each other to the meeting time. They become friends and develop a sense of community. Also, they spur each other on to grow in the faith and to reach out to unchurched people.

Cell groups meet outside the church building. Most often they gather in homes, but they could also meet in restaurants, parks, or work places. The location significantly influences the group's dynamics. A group that meets in the church building inevitably takes on a classroom or an "institutional" feel that can hinder personal transparency and warmth. Also, pre-Christians are not as comfortable entering a church building as they are going to a home or a restaurant. Since evangelism is one of the main functions of a cell group, the meeting place should help, not hinder, outreach. Meeting in homes also locates ministry in the midst of multiple neighborhoods, spreading the gospel across an area instead of stockpiling believers in a central building.

Although a cell group consists of more than a meeting, the quality of the meeting is vital. Cell meetings need to be life-giving experiences of Christ's presence and of transparent relationships. Meetings are more likely to hit that target if they are structured so that they encourage people to encounter God and each other.

One of the most common meeting formats used in cell-based churches is that of the "4 Ws". They are:

1. *Welcome*—getting acquainted.

2. *Worship*—exalting God through song or other means.

3. *Word*—study of the Scripture.

4. *Works*—ministering to one another and planning group activities.

However, this is not the only possible meeting format. The typical cell group meeting at Crossroads Church lasts about an hour and a half and follows this pattern:

1. *Ice Breaker:* Light-hearted questions designed to get people talking with one another.

2. *Vision Moments:* The group members discuss future plans, pray for unreached friends by name, and share about their evangelistic efforts.

3. *Applying the Scripture:* The group discusses questions designed to apply the Bible text which was taught in the weekend message. The group leader does not teach a lesson, but rather facilitates discussion of a set of questions that have been provided by the church for that week.

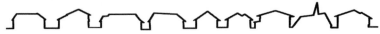

4. *Praying Together:* Group members pray for one another's needs. This is not a time to receive prayer requests for people outside the group. The question is a personal one: "How can we pray for you?" When people pray they experience God's presence. By praying for each other's needs, the members strengthen their relationship and express caring for one another. Members' faith grows as they see God answer prayer.

When a cell group is working right, members reach out to unreached people, experience true-life change, transparent community, and God's presence. It is exciting to be part of that kind of group; it is the church in action! (For more on the cell group, see chapter seven.)

The Worship Celebration

Even though cell groups may include worship in their meetings, corporate worship is an essential part of a cell church. One of the differences between house churches and cell churches is that house churches do not gather weekly with other groups for worship. Cell churches do. One way of looking at the weekly celebration service is to see it as the cell groups coming together to praise God and to celebrate what God is doing in their midst.

As in other churches, worship in a cell church is open to the public, so there may be many guests in attendance. Indeed, many members find their unchurched friends more receptive to an initial invitation to worship than to an invitation to a group meeting. At Crossroads we find that most (but not all) pre-Christians attend a worship service before they try a small group. Therefore, we seek to make each service encouraging to believers and understandable to guests. It is important for excellence and authenticity to characterize every celebration service. We do not advance the health of cell groups by settling for mediocrity in worship.

A cell church is not defined by worship style. As long as the worship format is meaningful to the people of the community, it really doesn't matter what kind of music or liturgy is used.

However, it is important to understand what we are trying to accomplish during a weekend worship time. For example, at Crossroads, we do not seek to build community on a Sunday morning. We have multiple services, and even if we serve coffee and donuts, people will not be able to truly share their lives during or between worship services. Certainly, members find and greet one another warmly at weekend services. But we are not structuring the services so as to promote fellowship. People will develop true community much better in cell groups. When it comes to the preaching, I do not try to disciple from the front. That is, I am not trying to meet all a believer's spiritual growth needs with my sermon. Discipleship is better done in a personal, relational (cell) context.

The goal of our weekend services is to glorify God. We also seek to inspire believers, and to invite pre-Christians to follow Christ.

Step 2: CONNECT[1]

Once people begin attending worship and/or a cell group, they need to become established in the faith and committed to the people and the vision of the church. At Crossroads, the two ways we accomplish this are through the Newcomers Class and the Encounter Retreat.

Newcomers Class

Not all cell churches would include this component in their strategy, but it is an important one at Crossroads. The Newcomers Class provides a practical first step for people who are new to the church. Participants learn about the vision and values of the church, and if they have not already done so, they are given the opportunity to make a commitment to follow Christ. If they are not yet part of a cell group, they are encouraged to join one, and are given the chance to form a group right out of their class. Newcomers Class serves as the membership class for Crossroads Church. It allows us to paint a clear picture of Crossroads as a cell-based church, which increases our congregational unity. However, the emphasis of the class is not on institutional enrollment or on membership privileges. Newcomers Class is about helping people take another step in their spiritual journey; a journey that may result in membership, but certainly does not end there. Membership just sets the stage for further growth. One of the commitments we ask of all new members is to attend the Encounter Retreat.

Encounter Retreat

At this life-changing overnight retreat, believers experience the love and grace of Christ in a very personal and powerful way. The retreat focuses on the power of the cross, enabling participants to drop the "baggage" of past hurts, guilt, and hang-ups.[2] Participants return from these retreats highly energized spiritually. At the end of the retreat many will sign up for the

School of Discipleship so that they can become group leaders. (See chapter seven for more details.)

Step 3: EQUIP

Martha's spiritual growth started when she began worshiping and participating in a cell group. Her growth continued as she attended an Encounter Retreat. But her spiritual maturity rose to a new level when she started to lead a group and minister to others.

Cell-based churches want to help all believers grow and become cell leaders. (For more on why this is so, see chapter six.) Two important ways believers are equipped to become group leaders are by serving as an apprentice and through the School of Discipleship.

Apprentice

The first stage of becoming a group leader is to serve as an apprentice. This part of the leadership training is highly personalized. An apprentice receives on-the-job training by sharing the group ministry with the leader. Under the supervision of the leader, the apprentice will lead the discussion questions, make follow-up phone calls, and generally share the responsibility for the group. The leader provides feedback and encouragement, knowing the apprentice will eventually become a group leader, too. The apprentice role is a transitional role, not a permanent one.

School of Discipleship

The School of Discipleship is a group leadership training course. Its purpose is to provide the vision and knowledge group members need to become group leaders. It is taught around the weekend service times so as not to interfere with cell meetings. The instructors are experienced group coaches who have teaching gifts.

The School consists of three modules, each thirteen weeks long. The School teaches the church's vision, the basics of the faith, a biblical overview, and the nuts and bolts of cell group leadership. By the time students graduate from the School they are leading a group themselves. (See chapter seven, page 92 for more details on the School of Discipleship.)

Step 4: SEND

When Martha became a group leader, her own group leader Barb became

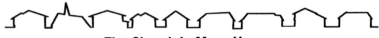

her coach. As a result, Martha's relationship with Barb was preserved and deepened. Barb continued to care for and develop Martha, just as she did when Martha was serving as her apprentice.

At Crossroads, coaches are always "player-coaches"; that is, they not only minister to leaders, they also lead cell groups themselves. All leaders provide ministry to those in their cells, and they receive ministry from their coach. In this model, leaders will not burn out due to constant giving because they are also receiving. Also, no single individual will be caring for too many people. This structure is often called the "Jethro principle,"[3] named after Moses' father-in-law. Exodus 18 recounts that Jethro saw Moses being consumed with the demands of managing the problems of the entire nation. So Jethro encouraged Moses to divide the people into manageable groups, and then delegate the leadership responsibilities for each among capable individuals. When adapted to a church's cell group context, the essential principle is that every leader in the church provides and receives ministry to a limited number of people. The resulting structure looks something like this:

A Jethro Coaching Structure

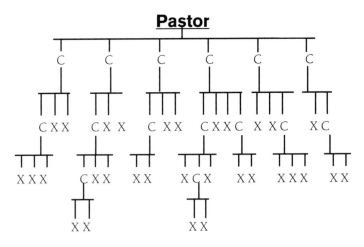

C=Coach & Group Leader
X=Group Leader

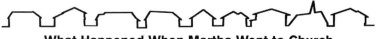
Coaching Groups

A "coaching group" (other churches use different names) is formed when a leader births a new group. The apprentice who was being trained on the job by the leader starts leading a separate group. The original leader now becomes the new leader's coach (see diagram below).

One additional note: As I finished this chapter, Martha pulled me aside after a worship service to show me the new engagement ring on her finger. She is now engaged to be married to another member of Crossroads Church! They have both found new life in Christ at Crossroads and are involved in cell ministry. They are committed and excited about building a Christ-centered life together. Life change, indeed!

TWO KINDS OF GROUPS

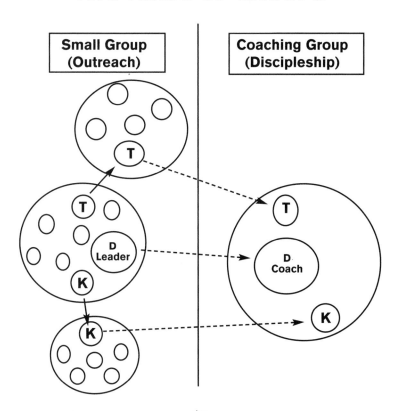

This system means group leaders participate in two kinds of groups: an open cell and a coaching group. Coaching is crucial to any group ministry, because an isolated group leader will eventually burn out. Coaches meet about twice per month with their leaders to provide encouragement, accountability, personal care, prayer, and teaching. Coaches are vital to cell "quality control," and they are trained to give personal attention to the personal and spiritual needs of their leaders. Since it takes time for coaches to maintain strong relationships with leaders, at Crossroads we try to limit to three the number of leaders coached by a single individual. (Full-time staff can coach many more, though.) If a leader develops more than three new leaders, the new leaders may be passed on to another coach for care and oversight.

In contrast to a cell group's outreach focus, the coaching group is focused on discipleship. The agenda of coaching-group meetings includes dealing with advanced topics of spiritual maturity, especially as they relate to group ministry. These topics would not be as appropriate to the open cell group.[4] A coaching group is not an open group in that new people are not invited in. A coaching group grows only when the coach's group multiplies and the new leader is added.

NOTES

1. Bethany World Prayer Center and ICM in Bogata use the term "consolidate."
2. Some cell churches prepare participants for the retreat with a "pre-Encounter class." And after the experience they offer another class ("post-Encounter"), which is designed to help people keep growing. At Crossroads the Newcomers Class serves as the "pre-Encounter" class.
3. The concept of the "Jethro Principle" was popularized by Carl George in his book *Prepare Your Church for the Future* (Tarrytown, NY: Fleming Revell Co., 1991).
4. Bill Hybels and Willow Creek Community Church are widely known for creating two kinds of weekly celebrations: one for spiritual seekers and one for believers. Through the Coaching Group (or "G-12" group) Cesar Castellanos and others did the same for the cell: created one group focused on outreach and the other on discipleship.

CHAPTER THREE

The Examples of
Jesus and Wesley

Airplanes can look quite different from one another. A radio-controlled model airplane, a commercial airliner, and a wedge-shaped stealth bomber may look radically different from one another, but they all fly because they utilize universal principles of aerodynamics.

Similarly, not all cell churches look exactly alike, but they thrive because they utilize timeless, biblically based ministry principles. Cell churches have not really invented a fundamentally new ministry approach. Rather, they have simply applied principles that have been used by Jesus and by the church throughout history.

Impact Through Others

There has been no other life that has had more of an impact on the world than that of Jesus Christ. Virtually everyone readily acknowledges that Jesus Christ changed the course of human history. Even our calendar is based on his birth.

The impact of Jesus' life is all the more remarkable when we consider that he never used a telephone, he had no Internet access, and never appeared on television or in a newspaper. Jesus never wrote a book, nor did he ever travel far from his home. How, then, did Jesus influence the world as he did?

Humanly speaking, Jesus' lasting impact came through the people he left behind. Jesus' strategy for changing the world was to train disciples who could make disciples of others. It wasn't Jesus himself who carried the message of the gospel to Rome and beyond, it was his followers who did so.

The gospel accounts show us that a large part of Jesus' ministry centered on training his followers to reach others with the Good News. Jesus' goal of making disciples who could make disciples was evident even as he called his first followers: "Jesus called out to them, 'Come, be my disciples, and *I will show you how to fish for people!*'" (Matthew 4:19 NLT, author's emphasis).

Jesus' goal was not to gather followers. Instead, Jesus' goal was to train twelve people to carry out his mission. Jesus was not upset or worried when the crowds started to desert him. His only question was whether or not his twelve would turn aside. In John 6:66-67 we read:

> From this time many of his disciples turned back and no longer followed him.

> "You do not want to leave too, do you?" Jesus asked the Twelve (NIV).

Though the crowds left Jesus, he knew his Twelve could eventually reach them again. But if the Twelve turned away there would have been no one equipped to carry on Jesus' mission once he left the earth.

Jesus' Disciple-Making Process

In his classic book, *The Master Plan of Evangelism*,[1] Robert E. Coleman analyzed the process Jesus used to create world-changing disciples. He found there were eight distinct steps in the process. In the New Testament these eight stages do not always fall in strict sequence. However, they do reveal that Jesus' disciple-making ministry followed a plan. The eight steps Coleman identified are:

1. *Selection.* When Jesus launched his public ministry, he selected twelve men to share it with him. Before he called those first disciples, Jesus spent all night in prayer, seeking God's guidance as to whom to select.

2. *Association.* Jesus spent a lot of time with those he called. His invitation was, "Come follow me." For three years Jesus and the Twelve lived together. They traveled by foot together, ate together, ministered together, experienced hardship, joy, acceptance, and rejection as a group. Jesus ministered to the crowds, but he spent most of his time with the Twelve. In fact, as his crucifixion approached, Jesus spent almost all his time with them.

3. *Consecration.* Jesus expected his disciples to be loyal and obedient learners. He asked for the disciples' hearts, and called them to develop his character.

4. *Impartation.* Jesus poured his life into his disciples, giving them his joy, his peace, and his authority. He gave them the Holy Spirit so that they would have the power to do what he asked them to do (John 20:22).

5. *Demonstration.* The disciples saw how Jesus lived and how he ministered to others. As the disciples watched, Jesus taught about the kingdom of God, and he demonstrated the kingdom by healing people physically and spiritually.

After this, Jesus traveled about from one town and village to another, proclaiming the good news of the kingdom of God. The Twelve were with him, and also some women who had been cured of evil spirits and diseases . . . (Luke 8:1-2 NIV).

6. *Delegation.* After Jesus let the disciples watch him teach and heal, he sent them out to do the very same things.

When Jesus had called the Twelve together, he gave them power and authority to drive out all demons and to cure diseases, and he sent them out to preach the kingdom of God and to heal the sick (Luke 9:1-2 NIV).

7. *Supervision.* Coleman observes: "Jesus made it a point to meet with his disciples following their tours of service to hear their reports and to share with them the blessedness in doing the same thing."[2] For example, after Jesus sent out the seventy-two to minister in the surrounding towns, he gathered them together again for a debriefing:

The seventy-two returned with joy and said, "Lord, even the demons submit to us in your name." He replied, "I saw Satan fall like lightning from heaven. I have given you authority to trample on snakes and scorpions and to overcome all the power of the enemy; nothing will harm you. However, do not rejoice that the spirits submit to you, but rejoice that your names are written in heaven" (Luke10:17-20 NIV).

In essence, Jesus gave his disciples "on the job" coaching.

8. *Reproduction.* Finally, Jesus expected his disciples to make other disciples and thus reach the world. If one disciple won and equipped another person to Christ, and then both of those believers won and equipped another person, the power of multiplication would soon spread the gospel widely.

Then Jesus came to [his disciples] and said, "All authority in heaven and on earth has been given to me. Therefore go and make disciples of all nations, baptizing them in the name of the Father and of the Son and of the Holy Spirit" (Matthew 28:18-19 NIV).

How did Jesus' followers know how to go make disciples? They knew because Jesus had just made disciples of them! They could replicate the process Jesus had used with them.

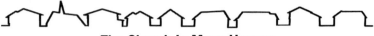

Applying Jesus' Master Plan

As a seminary student, I was privileged to study under Dr. Coleman. I read *The Master Plan of Evangelism* and I was captivated by the multiplication power of making disciples who can make disciples. I had visions of starting a spiritual "chain reaction" of discipleship.

However, I was not very good at applying Jesus' principles. When I started as pastor of my first church after seminary, I asked a young man to meet with me regularly, hoping to disciple him. Although we talked about the Scripture and our life in Christ, I didn't provide a clear direction or goal. I am sure that my young friend had no clue as to what I was hoping would happen through our time together. Eventually, we stopped meeting and I turned my full attention to developing the programs of the church. Looking back, I see that I needed a format that would have provided focus and support for helping my friend become a disciple who made disciples.

Cell-based ministry provides a practical way for local churches to build their ministries on the priorities and practices of Jesus. Without straining for an exact correlation, Jesus' eight disciple-making steps are recognizable in the cell church's ministry strategy. For example:

1. *Selection.* When group leaders (or members) invite someone to become part of their cell group they practice Jesus' selection principle.

2. *Association.* Spending time in and outside of group meetings is a cornerstone of group-based ministry. As members spend time with each other they build relationships.

3. *Consecration* is the principle of obedience to Jesus. The School of Leaders teaches people the ways of Christ, and calls them to yield to his Lordship. The Encounter retreat also challenges people to a deeper commitment to following Christ's ways.

4. *Impartation.* The Encounter retreat also provides an environment and avenue for people to open themselves to receiving the gift of God's Spirit.

5. *Demonstration.* Group members watch their leader minister both in the group meeting and throughout the week. Apprentices watch that example especially carefully since they are preparing to lead a group themselves.

6. *Delegation.* Group leaders regularly delegate ministry tasks to group members, and especially to their apprentices. Leaders learn never to

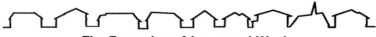

practice ministry alone, but to delegate as often and as much as possible. For example, a group leader might ask one group member to lead the opening prayer, another to call people that week to remind them about a change in meeting location, and still another member to organize meals for an ill group member.

7. *Supervision.* Group leaders coach their apprentices, and when the apprentices begin to lead groups of their own, the original leaders stay in a coaching relationship with them. The coaching relationship is one of supervision and encouragement.

8. *Reproduction.* The cycle is complete when new leaders are released and begin to multiply their groups and start their own coaching group, encouraging and discipling the new leaders they have developed.

How the Cell Church Applies Jesus' Master Plan

Jesus' Plan (Coleman)	Cell Church Ministry
Selection	Invite to small group
Association	Relationship with group members
Consecration	School of Leaders/Encounter
Impartation	Encounter retreat/School
Demonstration	Apprenticeship
Delegation	Apprentice-->group leader
Supervision	Coaching relationship
Reproduction	Building a coaching group

The cell church provides a practical framework for implementing the principles of Jesus' disciple-making strategy. As the modern cell church movement seeks to implement Jesus' strategy, it is important to note that it has worked before. About seventeen hundred years after Jesus another cell-based disciple-making movement helped change a nation.

A Nation Is Changed

In the eighteenth century, England was one of the most powerful nations in the world. Even so, turmoil was surfacing. The Industrial Revolution was causing huge economic change. There were a few who controlled the wealth, but many others were wretchedly poor. This was especially true in the cities.

Social ills and immoral behavior permeated society. Children as young as five years old were forced to work twelve-hour days in the mines and factories. Less than four percent of the total population had any schooling at all. Alcohol consumption was rampant. In 1736, one out of every six houses in London was licensed as a grog shop. Drunkenness was shredding the self-worth of the working people, leaving them hopeless. Britain was also running the world's slave trade. On top of that, those who owed money could be put in debtor's prison and sold into indentured servitude.[3]

While the governing classes projected an image of dignified prosperity, the majority of the English population was reeling with poverty, disease, and moral decay. This proved to be a volatile social recipe, as seen in France in the latter part of the century when this kind of social unrest boiled over into a revolution. England seemed to be ripe for a similar social explosion.

Unfortunately, the church did not seem to be a source of help. By and large, the state-sponsored Church of England was not connecting with the common people. There was very little spiritual passion in the clergy or the people.

It was in this environment that John Wesley started to preach a message of personal faith in Christ. Once a discouraged and searching young clergyman, he had personally experienced the assurance of God's pardon while attending a small group Bible study. As a result, he felt compelled to preach salvation by grace through faith. Wesley's goal was nothing less than to change society. He declared that his mission (and that of his followers) was "to spread scriptural holiness across the land."

At first Wesley spoke only in churches, but then he was convinced to take

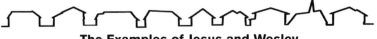

the message directly to the common people. He preached everywhere he could find listeners—to miners on their way to work in the morning, or to villagers in the town squares. People were converted by the hundreds and then by the thousands.

Soon, Wesley started organizing the new converts into home-based small groups (which he called "classes"). Lay people led fellow believers in encouraging each other to apply Bible teachings, care for one another, and welcome new members.

The combination of field preaching and small group ministry produced powerful results. Eventually, the message of the Gospel, along with this system of interlocking groups, spread all across England. As people were converted and the groups multiplied, towns were transformed. By the end of the eighteenth century, the nation of England had been deeply affected by what became known as the Wesleyan Revival. French historian Elie Halevy, among others, credits the Wesleyan movement with preventing a violent revolution like the one France endured.[4] At the time of his death, Wesley left behind one hundred thousand members in a network of ten thousand interlocking groups that became known as the Methodist Church.

Wesley's Method

The two main pillars of the Methodist movement were the same two employed by the cell church: celebration and cell. Wesley centered his ministry on the large group gathering, (which, besides the Anglican worship service, included a preaching event called the "Society"), and the small group gathering (the "class"). By the end of Wesley's life both Societies and classes had spread throughout England. As a result, the spiritual temperature of England was profoundly changed.

The Class

John Wesley borrowed and developed the idea of the small group from Reformation pioneers and from the Scriptures. He came to believe that one's spiritual vitality depends on one's participation in a Christ-centered small group.

Despite their name, these were not classes geared to instruction. They were actually highly interactive small groups, which focused specifically on behavioral change. Class members were to share their personal spiritual progress and problems, and the result was life change. Some of the questions used regularly in the meetings were:

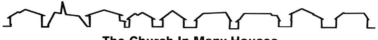
1. What known sins have you committed since our last meeting?

2. What temptations have you met with?

3. How were you delivered?

4. What have you thought, said, or done of which you doubt whether it be sin or not?[5]

Clearly, the point of the class was not the acquiring of information, but rather mutual encouragement in living out the faith.

Wesley felt so strongly about the need for new converts to be in class that he would not even preach anywhere he could not also start classes. Membership in a class was taken quite seriously. There was no such thing as a Methodist without a class. Only after faithfully attending a class for three months could one become a member of a Methodist society. In fact, Wesley said, "Those who will not meet in class cannot stay with us."[6] The first step toward any level of leadership in the Methodist movement started with leadership in the class.

John Wesley was not the only leader in the revival that swept England in the eighteenth century. George Whitefield was a key figure as well. In fact, Whitefield was widely regarded as a more dynamic preacher than Wesley. But Wesley's influence lived on long after he died because of the way he organized his ministry. Wesley's combination of large group and small group gatherings not only helped converts grow spiritually, they also helped the Wesleyan movement grow and endure. Eventually, Whitefield realized this. Later in life he reflected:

> My brother Wesley acted wisely—the souls that were awakened under his ministry he joined in class, and thus preserved the fruits of his labor. This I neglected, and my people are a rope of sand.[7]

The Society

The Society was a large group meeting that gathered all the Methodists (and those who responded to the field preaching) of a given area. The function of the Society was instructional teaching. In many ways, the Society was like a local congregation, in that it was a gathering of several groups and a center of spiritual identity. At Society meetings preachers lectured to the listeners who were seated in rows. Unlike the class, the Society meeting was not designed to be interactive. The main goal at this large group gathering was to disseminate the practical spiritual truth the Methodists were expected to live out.

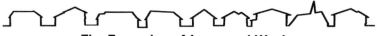

Wesley's Structure and the Cell Church		
Wesley's Structure	Function	Modern Cell Equivalent
Anglican Church	Worship	Weekend Services
Society	Teach Information	Weekly Sermons and School of Discipleship
Class meeting	Alter Behavior (Application of Bible)	Open cell group

A Motivating Purpose

In the midst of this discussion of ministry structure, it is important to note the unifying theme of this chapter: that of changing the world. Jesus' purpose was nothing less than changing the world by ushering in the kingdom of God. He was not merely trying to start or enlarge an organization. Jesus passed his mission on to his followers, saying ". . . go and make disciples . . ." (Matthew. 28:19 NIV). John Wesley also sought to change the world. His stated purpose was to "spread scriptural holiness across the land." Wesley developed his methods with that goal in mind. As a result, he helped to change England (and the United States).

All local churches are to be God's instruments for changing the world by making disciples through the power of the Holy Spirit. This perspective is central to the cell church, because the cell church approach will work *only* when a congregation's purpose is to reach society and have an impact upon it. M. Scott Boren asserts, "Cell groups do not work as a maintenance strategy. They only work when they exist to change the world."[8]

If you are looking for a way to keep church members happy, then I would not advise you to adopt the cell-based approach. However, perhaps your heart yearns to see the kingdom of God break in on this broken world. Maybe you are captured by a vision of a society that is more like the one God intended. Maybe you are unwilling to accept the fact that there are many people in your community who are living far from God, cut off from true hope, love, and wholeness.

If you dare to believe that God's will for your church goes beyond survival or even numerical growth, you can take heart from the cell-based churches that are being used by God to change their communities. Any congregation that shares Wesley's passion for fulfilling Jesus' Great Commission will find that cell ministry is a practical, biblical strategy for equipping and releasing members to reach the world.

NOTES

1. Robert E. Coleman, *The Master Plan of Evangelism* (Grand Rapids, MI: Fleming Revell, 1963).

2. Ibid., 89.

3. D. Michael Henderson, *John Wesley's Class Meeting* (Nappanee, IN: Evangel Publishing House, 1997), 17-20.

4. Ibid., 29.

5. David Lowes Watson, *The Early Methodist Class Meeting* (Nashville, TN: Discipleship Resources, 1985), 201.

6. Wesley's Letters Vol. 7, 154.

7. Henderson; *John Wesley's Class Meeting*, p. 30 – quoting Holland M. McTyeire, History of Methodism (Nashville, TN: Publishing House of the M. E. Church, South, 1904), 204.

8. M. Scott Boren, *Making Cell Groups* Work (Houston, TX: Cell Group Resources, 2002), 35.

Part II
Laying the Foundations

CHAPTER FOUR

The Challenge of Thinking Differently

"Although not all change is the same, there is one common element to change, and that is thinking."[1]
  —*John Maxwell,*
   quoting from the book The Seven Levels of Change

"Cell [ministry] is the challenge to move into a new mindset, or
maybe regain the one God always intended."[2]
    —*Chris Neal in* Church Without Walls

I was standing near the airport baggage claim area, scrutinizing people as
they moved past me toward the accumulating pile of luggage. I was trying
to spot a specific passenger, a man who was to visit our church. The problem was I had never met this man before, and I had only a small picture to
help me identify him. Unfortunately, no one seemed to match my snap-
shot. Eventually, most of the crowd drifted away from the baggage carousel
and there were only a few people left. After a few minutes one of them
approached me and tentatively called my name. It was my passenger! I
hadn't recognized him, but he had recognized me. It turns out that the picture I was carrying had been taken years earlier, and he had significantly
changed his appearance since that time. I had let my passenger walk right
past me because he did not match my picture of him.

Most people, especially longtime church members, carry a mental picture
of "church." Just as a mosaic is made up of many small pieces of colored
material artistically arranged to form an image, a cluster of assumptions
forms our picture of "church." Based on our experiences, we form
assumptions about the nature of ministry, the role of leaders, basic expectations of members, and so on. We may not even be aware of our presuppositions, but they profoundly influence us anyway.

In many ways, cell-based ministry looks quite different than the picture of
church most of us carry. That is why, when first exposed to the cell
church, we may say to ourselves, "That doesn't look quite right. That is

not how a church is supposed to work." So, without knowing it, we might pass by the kind of church we are really looking for.

Small groups had been a vital part of Crossroads' ministry strategy even before we switched to the cell model. Because of this, I had naively believed that we could make a few structural shifts and operate as a cell church before people even noticed. After all, since we already valued groups, how hard could it be to make a few changes and take our ministry to another level? Harder than I thought, I discovered.

During our transition to the cell strategy, there were several occasions when we experienced resistance from some of our members. A few in the congregation said they were uncomfortable with the cell model but couldn't explain why. Some felt we were placing too much emphasis on numbers. Still others did not find the Bible teaching format they wanted. As we talked together it became apparent that there was an underlying root to these concerns, which went far deeper than their face value. Those who were concerned were good people who loved God, and wanted to know and serve the Lord better. Though I tried to point out that the cell approach was the best way to accomplish precisely those aims, not everyone was convinced. Where was the disconnect?

No doubt part of the answer is that I could have done a better job of casting vision and explaining the change. However, I also came to realize that a conflict of assumptions was at the core of the resistance. Cell ministry is not really about structure and method. It is about values. It is driven by a specific way of thinking about the church. Conflict arose because the assumptions upon which cell ministry are based are quite different than those of the program-based church of which all of us have been part.

Examining Our Assumptions

Erwin McManus says, "Many leaders make the mistake of beginning with *what* rather than *why*, so the *what* is quickly rejected."[2] When leading a congregation toward cell-based ministry, we need to begin with the "why." We must understand and internalize foundational cell principles.

The biggest difference between a program-based church and a cell-based church is not the existence of small groups. A church can have dozens of small groups and still be thoroughly program-based. The biggest difference between a program-based and a cell-based church lies in the understanding of ministry upon which the church is built. That is why establishing cell structures and procedures is just part of the transition process. Transitioning to a cell-based ministry also requires a fundamental change in our thinking about ministry. Making this change is neither a quick nor an easy task.

One leader who was visiting our church told me he had been on the staff of two different churches that had "taken a stab" at cell ministry. Neither church transitioned successfully, and both quickly abandoned the experiment. I was not surprised at this outcome. If a church simply "takes a stab" at cell ministry, it probably will not work. Cell ministry requires a reformation of thinking, and that cannot happen overnight. When resistance to the transition arose in our church, I reminded myself that it had taken me several years to fully understand and embrace the cell model. I needed to give others time to process it, too.

Some contend that the cell church model will not work in North America. It has been said that although cell ministry seems to work well in other cultures, our culture is not conducive to the cell model. American independence, busyness, and relational distance from one another are thought to work against the success of cell ministry. However, it is not our culture but our mindset that most determines whether the cell model will work. Indeed, the cell approach can (and does) work in North America *if* certain assumptions about spiritual growth and the nature of the church are reexamined and renewed. There are five essential philosophical shifts program-based churches need to make in order for the cell approach to succeed. These are:

1. From "growing deeper" to "reaching outward"

2. From membership to disciple-maker

3. From educating to equipping

4. From programs to relationships

5. From a church with cells to a church that is cells.

There are many reasons a church might fail in its attempt to become cell-based. But one recipe for failure is for leaders to start building a cell structure before the people have made the shift to a cell philosophy. If church members have program-based assumptions about what it means to be a mature believer, what spiritual growth looks like, how people are won to Christ, and what the church should look like, then trying to impose a cell structure is destined to fail. However, if people inwardly make these five philosophical shifts, the cell approach will seem natural and right. The result will be effectiveness and unity.

In the next several chapters we will examine each of the five key shifts mentioned above. As we prepare to take a fresh look at commonly held assumptions, it might be helpful for you to pause and take a brief personal inventory of what you currently believe about topics such as:

Church: When someone says the word "church," what image comes to your mind? Some may see a building. Others may picture a worship service, or possibly acts of service to the poor. What is your dominant image?

At your church, what does it mean to be "active"? Does it mean attending worship services? Volunteering in service in the church or community? Something else? What do you think of when someone says they "go to church"?

Church Membership: When one is a member of a church, to what do they belong? An organization? A family? A mission?

Ministry: What does it mean to be in ministry? What kind of activities does it involve? Who does ministry? How are people prepared to do ministry?

Spiritual Growth and Maturity: What exactly does it mean to grow spiritually? What does spiritual maturity look like?

Processing these questions can help us begin to identify our presuppositions about church, and allow us to examine them more freely. But after we identify our assumptions, we might also ask ourselves *why* we believe what we do about these subjects. How biblical are our assumptions?

Anchoring Images

Reexamining and shifting our mindsets about spiritual matters not only takes time, it can be disorienting. For those who have been part of program-based churches for their entire spiritual lives, shifting to cell-based thinking can be like trying to adjust to living in a foreign land. Chris Neal said, "Moving into a new mindset is like moving into a new house. Some of your old furniture may come with you, but it will be in different surroundings, so it will look and feel different—and might even be put to new use." [4] The mindset shifts presented in the next few chapters might make ministry, discipleship, and spiritual growth "look and feel different" to you. If so, be patient. Allow yourself some time to get reoriented as you consider whether these mindset shifts might be biblically rooted. As you do, the following images might help you keep your balance.

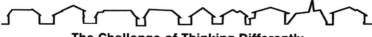

Cell church as ancient/future church

The cell church model is not a new approach to church. Although it works in the twenty-first century, it was not born as a reaction to our times. The cell church model is consistent with the nature of the ancient church, and it is also effective in today's world.

Our society may be changing around us, but little has changed within us. Technology continues to advance at dizzying speeds, changing the way we work, play, communicate, and learn. Major political changes have altered world alliances and the balance of power. Nonetheless, all human beings still have a deep need to be in relationship with God and with others. The priorities of the cell church focus on meeting those deep, unchanging needs. In many ways, shifting to a cell ministry mindset does not spur the church to keep up with the times; they help the church become independent of them.

Church as resident aliens

Some have said that the reason huge churches emerged in Africa, Asia, and South America is that those cultures are more suited to the cell model. Asian respect for authority and South American prioritization of personal relationships are thought to make people more open to the cell model. On the other hand, North American cultural values are often believed to be unfriendly to cell ministry.

While the growth of the world's huge cell churches cannot be explained simply in cultural terms, there is some truth to this observation. Cell ministry can cut against the grain of our American radical individualism, entertainment orientation, and consumerism. For example, we Americans are a busy people, and cell ministry takes time. Cell ministry won't work if faith is considered an optional activity, or as one more avenue to self-actualization. It is a lifestyle commitment that may not be reinforced by American values.

The question becomes: How biblical are North American values? Throughout history we see that the effectiveness of Christ's Church does not depend on how closely it reflects cultural values. The Bible calls us strangers and aliens in the world (1 Peter 2:11), and urges us not to be shaped by the world (Romans 12:2). Just because cell ministry cuts against the grain of our culture does not mean we should discard it. In fact, it might be one more reason to embrace it.

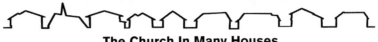

Church as furnace

It is difficult to describe the shift to a cell ministry mindset without contrasting it with the program-based model. However, I want to be clear that in the following chapters I am not branding the program-based church as useless and bankrupt. Millions of people have met Christ and grown spiritually in program-based churches.

Instead, we can think of the church as a furnace. Any working furnace will produce heat, but some are more efficient than others. The point is not that the program-based church will not produce any heat (disciples). However, when it is working right, the cell-based church is the most efficient way of making disciples who make disciples. That is why the world's largest churches are cell-based churches.

As the spiritual temperature of our society continues to drop, it is vital that the church be as effective as possible. The program-based church is not so much wrong as it is handicapped. By relying heavily upon the large gathering (the worship service) it is flapping only one wing. It is not able to fly as high as God intends and as the world needs. The cell ministry mindset and model may be different than what we are accustomed to, but then again, we are looking for results that are different than what we have seen. I encourage you to approach the following chapters with an open mind, not evaluating these ideas against past church experiences, but by what God calls the Church to become.

NOTES

1. From Maxwell's *Leadership Wired*, Col. 6 Issue. 2.
2. *Church Without Walls*, ed. Michael Green, (Carlisle, UK: Paternoster Press, 2002), 82.
3. Erwin Raphael McManus, *An Unstoppable Force* (Loveland, CO: Group Publishing, 2001), 195.
4. *Church Without Walls*, 82.

CHAPTER FIVE

Moving from "Growing Deeper" to "Reaching Outward"

"We encourage Christians and churches round the world not to focus on their own needs and desires! If you do, you will surely shrivel up and die."

—Chinese house church leaders

"Group outreach is the heartbeat of cell ministry."[1]

—Joel Comiskey

On April 15, 1912, the Titanic struck an iceberg in the North Sea and began taking on water. In the midst of the escalating chaos, some of the huge ship's passengers were hurriedly loaded into lifeboats. The twenty lifeboats lowered into the water that night were less than two-thirds full, and all had room for more people. Even though they heard cries for help, those in the boats rowed away from the nearly fifteen hundred people who were bobbing in the frigid water. They were afraid to row toward the drowning people for fear the large number of desperate victims would overwhelm and sink their lifeboats.

Like all the others, Fifth Officer Harold Lowe had rowed his Lifeboat #14 away from the panicked cries until he had reached a safe distance. But as he listened to the number of pleas for help become fewer and fewer, Lowe changed course. Lowe transferred his passengers into four other lifeboats, and then returned to the sinking ship to pick up more survivors. He was able to rescue an additional fourteen people from the water (though only half survived).[2]

Healthy cell groups are spiritual versions of Lifeboat #14. Just as Lifeboat #14's mission was to rescue as many persons as possible, the object of each cell group is to keep as many people as possible from sinking into meaningless, materialistic lives. Cell groups reach out to pre-Christians to offer new life in Christ.

Perhaps the biggest difference between program-based small groups and cell groups is that small groups are generally focused inward while cell groups are focused outward. Program-based small groups are usually avenues for Christians to "go deeper" through Bible study, prayer, and fellowship. Cell groups members study the Bible, pray together, and form close relational bonds, but a healthy cell is resolutely pointed out the door as well. Cell ministry is not about organizing the congregation into groups for better care; it is about reaching and discipling new believers. This outward emphasis does not hinder the spiritual growth of group members—it enhances it.

The Transforming Quest

In the popular book and movie trilogy, *The Lord of the Rings,* a small band of mythical creatures embarks on a quest to save the world. Their task is to destroy a magical ring, so that it can never fall into the possession of an evil entity that wants to use its power to rule Middle Earth.

A simple, good-hearted hobbit named Frodo is designated to carry the ring. A special team, the Fellowship of the Ring, is formed from creatures that would not normally associate with one another. Nonetheless, they pledge to help Frodo make the long, perilous journey to the only place the ring can be destroyed. The trilogy is the tale of their harrowing adventures.

By the end of the story, the characters have been personally changed as a result of their experiences. The members of the Fellowship have grown in character, bravery, wisdom, and self-control. They have learned about the world and about themselves.

The members of the Fellowship have also grown to be closer friends than they ever thought possible. For example, when facing a battle they could not win, two of the characters realized how much their relationship had changed.

Dwarf: "I never thought I would die fighting side-by-side with an elf!"

Elf: "What about side-by-side with a friend?"

Dwarf: (pauses, looking at the elf) "Aye, I could do that."

The quest was the key to all these personal changes. It was the challenge of destroying the ring that created the need for the Fellowship in the first place. It was the quest that thrust the characters into personal interactions out of which love grew. It was the quest that exposed them to situations that demanded more from them than they thought they possessed. With-

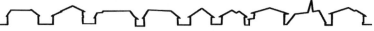

out the quest, not only would the ring have remained a danger to the world, the characters would not have grown as they did.

The Key to Spiritual Vitality

Each of us is created for a quest: We are called to participate in God's evangelistic mission in the world. As we join in this quest, we are deeply changed.

Evangelism is a constant theme running throughout the New Testament. The Gospels are the record of Jesus' work of announcing the Kingdom of God, and training his followers to do the same. The Gospel of Matthew concludes with Jesus commissioning his followers to act on their training, sending them to "go and make disciples of all nations" (Matthew 28:19). Next, the book of Acts chronicles the expansion of the quest. In the first chapter, the risen Jesus reminds his followers, "you will be my witnesses" (Acts 1:8). The rest of the book is the account of the early church fulfilling that evangelistic mandate. Most of the other New Testament books are letters written by evangelistic missionaries who instructed believers on how to live out their faith and influence a pagan society. Remove evangelism from the New Testament and there would be no Great Commission for which the twelve disciples train; the book of Acts would become the book of Sayings, and Paul would have had no mission churches to which he could write. Evangelism is central to the New Testament and to spiritual growth.

Groups and churches are healthiest when they pursue the quest to reach pre-Christians. As they share the love and Good News of Christ with others, they also grow spiritually. If a church allows evangelism to slip from the primary focus to a secondary activity, not only will the church's numerical growth slow down, but the church will also decrease in spiritual vitality.

In recent decades the church in China (especially the underground house church) has experienced extraordinary spiritual and numerical growth. In spite of persecution, thirty thousand Chinese per day come to faith in Christ. Even so, some Chinese leaders have become concerned that the nation's increasing financial prosperity could eventually dim the church's spiritual fervor. As they wrestled with this issue, they gained the following insight:

> When we brought our concerns before the Lord in prayer, he clearly showed us that the house churches of China will remain in revival

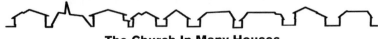

as long as they remain obedient to the vision to preach the gospel
. . . If we lose our first love and start to focus on our own needs, our
spiritual life will shrivel up and die. As long as we strive to obey
God's call to take the gospel to the Muslim, Buddhist, and Hindu
nations, he will bless our churches and revival will continue.[3]

The Mainspring of Cell Ministry

Outreach is the mainspring of a cell group. It is not the only purpose of
the cell group, but it needs the most emphasis because all groups have a
natural tendency to become comfortable and turn inward. We need to
remind leaders that if their groups do not reach out they will grow stagnant. Carl George writes:

> Show me a nurturing group not regularly open to new life, and I
> will guarantee it's dying. If cells are units of redemption, then no
> one can button up the lifeboats and hang out a sign, 'You can't come
> in here.' The notion of group members shutting themselves off in
> order to accomplish discipleship is a scourge that will destroy any
> church's missionary mandate.[4]

Most churches that emphasize reaching unreached people can expect to have
to answer the criticism that they are simply "after numbers." Now, it is certainly possible for churches to slip into an institutional mindset, driven by
ego to be the biggest. But focusing on fulfilling the Great Commission to
reach the unreached is not about hitting numerical quotas—it is about transforming lives. When the Titanic sank, the headlines read, "Fifteen hundred
souls lost." Were the newspaper editors simply interested in numbers? When
Officer Lowe turned Lifeboat #14 back toward drowning people, he told us
they rescued fourteen people. Someone counted. Why? Were they just interested in numbers? No, they were interested in people. Each number is a person, and each life reached is a destiny changed. Our passion to reach out
increases the more we internalize that truth.

Paradoxically, groups that focus on reaching others will also find themselves
growing closer to Christ and each other. Larry Kreider points out:

> The primary focus of each home cell group should be outreach and
> discipleship, rather than fellowship, although great fellowship will
> be a healthy by-product of the home cell group that is constantly
> reaching out to others.[5]

Just as those who serve together in the military often form special bonds,
believers who embark on a mission to reach unreached people grow quite

close to one another. As we pray for pre-Christian friends, take the risk of inviting others, and stretch ourselves spiritually, we can experience true community.

We need not fear that emphasizing outreach will weaken our spiritual depth. Reaching out to pre-Christian friends helps develop us spiritually as well. When we seek to share our faith, we gain a deeper grasp of it. When we deeply desire for our friends to know Christ, we are driven to pray for them. We are motivated to display the fruit of the Spirit when we know our lives must reflect Christ's character in order for our witness to be most effective.

It stands to reason that evangelism and discipleship would be closely connected. After all, discipleship is the process of becoming like Jesus, who was and is on a mission to the world! Jesus said, "For the Son of Man came to seek and to save what was lost" (Luke 19:10 NIV). In order to learn to follow Jesus, we need to go where he is going—into the world!

How Cells Reach Out

There are two main ways groups can reach out and grow numerically: 1) directly, by inviting unchurched pre-Christians to group meetings, or 2) indirectly, by inviting unconnected worship attenders to cells.

Direct outreach

In many cell churches around the world, cell attendance is actually higher than worship attendance. This is because group members invite their pre-Christian friends directly to the cell meeting and many are won to Christ in the cell context. It may take time for the newly converted person to start worshiping with the rest of the congregation. Direct cell outreach is very exciting because it decentralizes evangelism and makes each cell an entry point for new people. Instead of inviting pre-Christians to "come and see" a large event, Christians "go and show" the love of Christ to their networks of relationships. Through "go and show" evangelism cell members take the gospel into each apartment building, office, and housing plan in which members live and groups meet. This is sometimes called "penetration evangelism."

Indirect outreach

As desirable as it is, inviting pre-Christians directly to the group has not been the norm at Crossroads Church. We find that the majority of new people (though not all) attend a worship celebration before they attend a group. Most

unchurched people in our area are more open to an initial invitation to a weekend service than to a group meeting.

At each group meeting, members pray for their pre-Christian friends and families to be open to Christ. Then we encourage group members to invite their pre-Christian friends to a worship celebration. After they are attending worship regularly, they are more open to an invitation to a group meeting. We also challenge leaders to introduce themselves to those they meet at weekend services and to invite them to their groups. This indirect outreach is also very important, because worship attenders need to form relationships with other members in order to remain in the church and grow.

It is not necessary to choose between direct and indirect cell evangelism; a cell church can encourage both! It really doesn't matter whether a preChristian attends a worship service first or a group first. The goal is for everyone to participate in both.

Leading Cell Groups to Evangelize

A mainline church leader once emailed me, "I really like the idea of outreach-focused cell groups. But in my denomination most parishioners believe evangelism is the pastor's job. They seem terrified of inviting someone to worship. Will lay people really do this?"

Believers will reach out if they have: 1) the passion, 2) the training, 3) the determination, and 4) the prayer life to sustain their efforts. Leaders who want to increase the evangelistic temperature of their churches can start by addressing these four points.

1) Stir their passion for outreach.

If cell members have a strong desire to see people develop a growing relationship with Christ, they will reach out consistently. If they lack that passion, evangelistic progress will be slow.

The Apostle Paul had a passionate desire to see his fellow Jews come to faith in Christ. In Romans 9:2-3 he writes:

> My heart is filled with bitter sorrow and unending grief for my people, my Jewish brothers and sisters. I would be willing to be forever cursed—cut off from Christ!—if that would save them.

It was this kind of passion to see people come to Christ that propelled Paul to embark on his difficult missionary journeys. It is passion that will

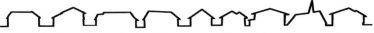

prompt a cell member to introduce herself to a visitor at worship, or to invite a co-worker to worship. Ultimately, this kind of passion comes from God. However, leaders can take some steps to help spark in their members the desire to reach out.

a) Teach the scriptural mandate for outreach.

Many Christians do not see evangelism as a part of the normal Christian life. Evangelism is seen as an activity best reserved for specialists, or perhaps a committee, or the pastor.

In fact, the longer a person is a believer, the more this is so. Surveys show that twice as many newer Christians as older (forty-two to twenty-one percent) strongly disagreed with the statement, "It's possible to be a committed Christian and not be active in telling others about Christ." Church consultant Bill Hull, author of *The Disciple Making Pastor*, says:

> I think this reflects the deadening effect of much institutional Christianity. When you have a pulpit-centered, institutional church model, where accumulating Bible knowledge and being involved in insulated programming shuts you off from the world, it desensitizes Christians to others' needs. There's an old axiom, "No contact, no impact."[6]

To counter this trend, leaders continually need to hold up the value of evangelism. At Crossroads we do this by regularly teaching on outreach at weekend services. Also, the School of Discipleship is laced with evangelism teaching and with sessions during which participants share their witnessing experiences.

b) Set the example.

If group members do not seem motivated to reach out, group leaders can become frustrated. They will ask, "I know the importance of outreach, but what if my group won't do it?"

I counsel these leaders, "Then you do it yourself!" I encourage them to tell the group who they are seeking to reach, and then to enlist the group's prayer support. Then, at future meetings, the leaders give updates on how their outreach efforts are going. And, of course, it is important to share the victories. This way the group gets involved in the action. Eventually, some will follow the leader's example and start witnessing, too. At the very least, the leader can train any newly won people in an outreach mentality and renew the group that way.

c) Share the results.

Nothing motivates like results! At Crossroads we frequently invite individuals to share with the worshiping congregation the story of how Christ is changing their lives. These stories are very uplifting and they can remind everyone of what really counts. One story of authentic life change can produce more faith sharing than a dozen sermons.

2) Train believers how to reach out.

Passion without training leads to frustration. Many Christians would be delighted to lead someone to Christ, but they do not know how to go about it. Therefore they conclude they should serve the church in other ways and leave the evangelism to others.

While not all have the gift of evangelism (I don't), each of us can give witness to our faith. One does not need the gift of evangelism in order to witness any more than one needs the gift of helps in order to move tables after a church function. Witnessing simply means sharing our faith stories, and if we are trained, each of us can do that.

One time-tested format for training individual believers to share their stories is to ask them to think through the following three prompts:

    a. Before I followed Christ . . .

    b. How I started following Christ . . .

    c. Since I followed Christ . . .

At Crossroads' School of Discipleship we invite participants to practice telling their personal stories to fellow classmates. This prepares them to share it more naturally with a pre-Christian as the opportunity arises. We are not trying to entice members simply to recite a pre-arranged speech. The goal is to equip people to share the reason for the hope that is within them (1 Peter 3:15).

Cell groups also benefit from adopting an intentional outreach strategy. One approach, based on Dale Galloway's, is as follows:

    a) Make a list.

Groups make a list of people they want to see come to the group and to faith in Christ. These could be names of people who are already attending worship but not a group, or they could be people who are not following Christ at all. This helps people get specific.

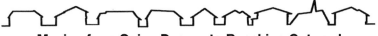

b) Pray for the people on the list.

After identifying specific unreached individuals, group members pray for them by name during the weekly meetings. Members also pray privately for these people outside the meeting.

c) Demonstrate Christ's love.

Believers build genuine friendships with those they hope to reach. Sometimes cells hold social gatherings to which they invite those on their prayer list. When people have fun with group members it increases the chances they will respond to an invitation to a group meeting later on.

Since many veteran Christians do not have many pre-Christian friends, they may need to take steps to make some! During the group meetings leaders can ask for members to share any experiences they had showing Jesus' love in practical ways. It is important to celebrate the simple acts of friendship.

d) Share your story.

Especially when reaching out to pre-Christian, believers can look for an opportunity to share their faith stories in a natural and relaxed manner.

e) Invite the list.

Group members invite their friends to either the worship celebration or to the group meeting, depending on which invitation would most likely be accepted. The goal is to get people involved in both celebration and cell, but it doesn't matter which one comes first.

3) Encourage them to persevere.

While this plan sounds simple enough to follow, results are not always instant. At times we need to remind cell members not to take a declined invitation as a personal rejection. Wise leaders will celebrate their members' outreach efforts even when they do not bear immediate results.

4) Highlight the need to pray.

Only God can change hearts. Therefore, consistent prayer both in and outside the meeting is essential. Members can pray for God to show them who is open to the love and message of Christ. It requires determination to keep praying, caring, and inviting others, but the payoff is worth it!

Stacy prayed, cared, and finally invited her friend Diane to her group.

Stacy's cell leader e-mailed me:

> Diane came back tonight for the second time. During the application of the scriptures discussion time, when we were sharing about how someone has been a "God reflector" to us personally, Diane recognized Stacy as her God reflector. She was so grateful that Stacy had become friends with her that she actually started to cry because she was so touched. I then shared with her that we had been praying for her since January, and she was just blown away.

> It was really exciting to see the benefits of praying the list, seeing God do His work. This whole incident has really helped this group . . . and it also goes to show that the more time I as a leader spend praying, the more God blesses the group!

The most effective cell churches see their mission as nothing less than reaching their city for Christ. Cell ministry is a city-taking strategy; it will not work if it is seen as simply a membership care tactic.

When we join God's great quest to reach others, we can become a church in which "every day they continued to meet together in the temple courts. They broke bread in their homes and ate together with glad and sincere hearts, praising God and enjoying the favor of all the people. And the Lord added to their number daily those who were being saved" (Acts 2:46-47 NIV).

NOTES

1. Joel Comiskey, *Home Cell Group Explosion* (Houston, TX: Touch Publications), 70.
2. I first saw the Lifeboat #14 illustration online at an unknown source I now cannot locate, though details of the actions of Harold Lowe, taken from Titanic-Titanic.com website; Kupy 2004.
3. Paul Hattaway, *Back to Jerusalem* (Waynesboro, GA: Gabriel Publishing, 2003), 104.
4. Carl George, *Prepare Your Church for the Future* (Grand Rapids, MI: Baker Book House, 1991), 99. and quoted by Joel Comiskey in Home Cell Group Explosion.
5. Larry Kreider, *House to House* (Ephrata, PA: House to House Publications, 1995), 85.
6. Craig Brian Larson, *Leadership*, Vol. 12, no. 4.

CHAPTER SIX

Moving from Member to Disciple-Maker

". . . we are the sheep of God, and sheep require the Shepherd to feed them, but there must come a time when we become shepherds who feed others."[1]

—*Erwin McManus*

"Jesus called out to them, 'Come, be my disciples, and I will show you how to fish for people!'"

—*Matthew 4:19, NLT*

Early in my ministry I served as pastor to a traditional, program-based church. It was made up of faithful, generous people, and had a strong Sunday School emphasis.

Though there were several fine adult classes, a number of young adults approached me to say they were anxious to start a new class for people their age. So, I identified some classroom space and a curriculum. The only remaining need was a teacher. I decided to ask a member of an older adult class to teach the new one. What better way to help young adults to follow Christ than to have older adults pass on what they have learned?

However, the first adult class member I asked turned down my request. He said, "I could never do that, I don't know enough about the Bible." So I approached a different member of the class and received the same answer: "I don't know enough about the Bible." As I reflected on their responses, I thought to myself, "They've been in that Sunday School class for nearly fifty years. When *will* they know enough about the Bible?" (I didn't say this. I may have been young and naïve, but I wasn't entirely stupid!)

I am not criticizing those sincere Christians for feeling unprepared to help others grow. This incident could have taken place at virtually any American church. Too often, churches settle for making attenders and listeners instead of producing disciples who make disciples. Therefore, most church members consider helping others grow spiritually to be beyond the call of "normal" Christian living.

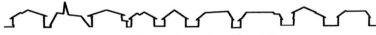

Redefining "Normal" Christianity

Most churches' purpose statements include language indicating that their mission is to make disciples (or "fully-devoted followers of Christ"). If making disciples is our goal, how do we know when we have one? What does a mature disciple look like? Of all the various habits and character traits commonly used to describe a mature Christian, one of the least mentioned is the ability to produce and equip other believers.

Biologically, an organism is physically mature when it can reproduce. Similarly, spiritual maturity includes the ability to spiritually "reproduce"! That is, mature believers are disciples who can make disciples. They are able to influence others toward Christ and to help them grow in the faith. This is not the only indicator of spiritual maturity, but it is an important one.

If the ability to make disciples of others is one of the markers of spiritual maturity, we would expect to find this "reproduction" principle in the New Testament. And, in fact, we do. For example, in 2 Timothy 2:1, Paul urges his young protégé Timothy:

> You then, my son, be strong in the grace that is in Christ Jesus. And the things you have heard me say in the presence of many witnesses entrust to reliable men who will also be qualified to teach others (NIV).

Paul was challenging Timothy to go beyond making believers; he was to equip believers to pass on their faith to others.

Likewise, the Gospels tell us that Jesus' goal was to teach his disciples to make disciples of others. When Jesus called his first followers, he made known his intent from the outset: "Jesus called out to them, 'Come, be my disciples, and I will show you how to fish for people!'" (Matthew 4:19 NLT).

Timothy and other early Christ-followers may have been called to make disciples. But does that mean all followers of Jesus should do so today? Are we each called to make disciples?

Most cell churches answer that question with an emphatic, "Yes." A cell church's ministry strategy is sharply focused on helping each believer become a disciple maker. And since reaching and discipling others is the "job description" of a cell leader, many cell churches state that their goal is to develop each member into a cell leader.

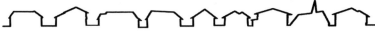

However, many members of program-based churches resist the idea of becoming cell leaders. One reason for this resistance is many church members have not been taught to think of spiritual reproduction as part of "normal" Christianity. They have been trained to be members instead of disciple-makers. Therefore, they are comfortable with membership activities such as attending worship regularly, believing the basic doctrine of the church, contributing money, living a moral life, and serving where they are needed and able. By regarding each church member as a potential cell leader, cell churches are redefining the popular understanding of discipleship. They communicate that it is "normal" for Christ's followers to share their faith and grow to the point they can help someone else grow.

Another reason program-based church members may push back against the idea of becoming group leaders is they may not believe they are capable of leading a group. They see cell leadership as a unique role reserved for those who are specifically called to that role. When challenged to lead a cell they respond, "Leading a group is not my gift," or, "I'm not the leadership-type."

Moving from a membership mentality to a disciple-making mindset requires a huge shift in thinking. In order to make that shift, we need to see cell leadership as a basic Christian activity, and that leading a cell is not beyond the ability of "normal" Christians.

Cell leadership is basic Christian living

Some ministries are common to all believers, while others are not. That is because some ministries are gift-based, while others are expressions of our common calling and character as Christians. For instance, every believer is called to pray, to love, and to give. Not all Christians are called to pastor, to teach, or to administrate.

If people see cell groups as just one of many possible church programs, they will probably regard group leadership as a specialized ministry. As a result, they will resist the suggestion that everyone should become a group leader. On the other hand, if people understand that a cell leader's role is simply to help others grow in the faith, and that all Christians can do that, then they regard cell leadership as open to all.

The New Testament teaches that helping others grow is not reserved for a select few. For example, Titus 2:3-5 says:

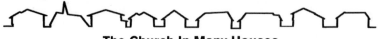

. . . tell the older women to be reverent in behavior, not to be slanderers or slaves to drink; they are to teach what is good, so that they may encourage the young women to love their husbands, to love their children, to be self-controlled, chaste, good managers of the household, kind, being submissive to their husbands, so that the word of God may not be discredited (NRSV).

This passage says that when it comes to teaching the younger women how to live out the Christian life, it is not the pastor or a uniquely gifted individual who is responsible for doing so; it is the older Christian women. The role of Titus (the pastor) was to equip the older women to fulfill that ministry.

Hebrews 5:12 suggests that helping others grow is expected for anyone who has been following Christ for a significant period of time:

In fact, though by this time *you ought to be teachers*, you need someone to teach you the elementary truths of God's word all over again. You need milk, not solid food (NIV, emphasis author's).

By telling these believers they need milk instead of solid food, the writer is telling his readers that they are not yet mature. The reason he knows they are immature is that they are not yet able to disciple others. Again, we see that helping others grow is part of a normal Christian activity. In fact, the inability to disciple others is cause for alarm.

Since discipling others is part of a normal Christian life, and since cell leadership is really nothing more than helping others grow, cell leadership is generally attainable for every follower of Christ. Though there will be exceptions to this rule, the vast majority of people in a congregation are capable of being trained to lead a cell. That is because cell ministry is based on spiritual maturity, not on spiritual giftedness.

Every believer is capable of becoming a group leader

The term "leader" can be intimidating. Some recoil at the idea of becoming a cell leader because they do not think of themselves as possessing leadership gifts. This is one of the limitations of using the title "leader." If I were starting our ministry over, I would consider using the title "cell servant" instead, because servanthood is the essence of group leadership. Cell leadership involves ministry tasks such as staying in touch with members, showing personal care, praying for members, listening, and sharing the faith. These are expressions of living out the faith more than they are of exercising the spiritual gift of leadership.

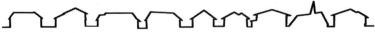

If group leaders were expected to be teachers, they would need the gift of teaching, and not everyone possesses that gift.[2] However, group leaders are not teachers. Since the Bible application segment of the group meeting is based on discussion questions distributed by the church, leaders do not teach, they facilitate discussion. If group leaders do not need the gifts of leadership or teaching, what characteristics are required? What does it take to be a good cell leader?

In order to find out, researcher Joel Comiskey surveyed seven hundred effective cell leaders (those who had multiplied their groups). He talked with leaders from five countries and three continents. In his book *Home Cell Group Explosion,* Comiskey reveals his findings.

First, Comiskey lists several factors that he discovered make no difference in one's ability to lead and multiply a group. These factors include traits such as gender, income, education or age. One might assume that the best cell leaders would be those with the spiritual gift of leadership. Not so! Comiskey discovered that there was no particular spiritual gift that made a leader more effective; persons with all types of gift-mixes multiplied cells. Personality made no difference, either. Both introverted and extro-verted leaders multiplied groups.

Factors which *do not* affect group multiplication:

❖ Leader's gender, income, age, marital status, or education

❖ Leader's personality type—both introverted and extroverted lead-ers multiply groups

❖ Leader's spiritual gifting—all types of gifting multiply groups[3]

However, there are some traits that do make a difference. Comiskey's research pinpointed several factors that are important to leading a group that multiplies. They are:

1. *Goals*—being able to state how and when their group would birth.

2. *Prayer*—leaders of multiplying groups prayed more than those who didn't multiply their groups.

3. *Training*—receiving training for their ministry.

4. *Contacts*—interactions and friendships with those outside the church.

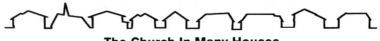
5. *Apprentices*—having recruited a leader-in-training. No apprentice, no multiplication.

6. *Care*—showing love to the group members.

Factors which *do* affect group multiplication:

- ❖ Prayer
- ❖ Goals
- ❖ Training
- ❖ Contacts
- ❖ Apprentices
- ❖ Care[4]

Virtually any Christ-follower can do the activities on this list! Caring and praying do not require special calling or gifting, merely the will and the desire. Comiskey's research demonstrates that there is no such thing as the gift of cell-leading. Any growing disciple is capable of leading a group.

Indeed, hundreds of years ago, the early Wesleyan class system was built on the principle that anyone can lead a group. Henderson writes:

> . . . one of the strengths of the Methodist concept of leadership [was]: it took no training or talent to be a class leader; anyone could do it. Being a class leader was in no way related to wealth or education or professional expertise or social standing; it was not an elite position. But it did demand faithfulness, honesty, and concern for people. Anyone who demonstrated these qualities as a class leader could rise to higher levels of leadership, but without them it was impossible to be a Methodist leader, no matter how educated or wealthy or talented.[5]

Once Christians realize they really are capable of discipling someone else, they might be surprised at how effectively they can lead a group.

Linda has been a faithful member of Crossroads Church since its inception. She has served in many ways: teaching in the children's ministry, singing on the worship team, assisting with office tasks, and more. She has also been a member of a cell group for many years.

Although Linda served in many ministries, she consistently declared, "One thing I'll never do is lead a group. I am not the leadership type and working with adults is just not my thing. I serve in other ways."

Eventually, Linda sensed God was prompting her to try leading a group. Much to her surprise, not only did she find she was helping others grow, but she also grew spiritually herself! Though she had been a dedicated Christ-follower for a long time, as she led her group Linda noticed new changes in her prayer life, character, and faith. She said, "I have grown in many ways that I know I wouldn't have had I not become a group leader."

Another result of leading a group that Linda did not expect was she influenced others to become leaders as well. Karen and her husband were members of Linda's group. One day her husband e-mailed me about Linda's quiet influence on them:

> After being a part of Linda's group for almost eight months now, [Karen] has seen leadership modeled every week. So when it came time for her to step up to it, it came very naturally to her. So, [Linda] has had a very positive influence through her leadership that has spun off to me and Karen as well!

For a long time Linda was sure she would never be a cell leader, but now she is a very effective one. Incidentally, I am quite familiar with Linda's story, because Linda is my wife!

Why a Cell Group's Goal is Multiplication

Healthy cell groups multiply. In chapter one, a cell group was defined as: "a group of three to fifteen people that meets weekly outside the church building for the purpose of evangelism and discipleship *with the goal of multiplication.*"

In the early days of Crossroads' transition to the cell model, some of our members became uncomfortable with multiplication being the goal of a group. They were concerned that we were trying to build impressive statistics, rather than minister to people.

Why is multiplication the goal of every cell group? Is it just about ego or inflating the church's numbers?

One reason groups need to multiply is that evangelism is central to the group's mission. As a group fulfills the Great Commission, it reaches out. When new people are won and added to the group, eventually the group will need to birth in order to keep from becoming too large.

However, there is another very important reason that multiplication is the goal of the group. A cell leader's goal is to lead each group member to become a fully devoted follower of Jesus. Since a mature disciple is one who can disciple someone else (which is the role of a group leader), then the goal of a leader is to help group members become group leaders. And when group members become group leaders, new groups are born! Therefore, the goal of the group is to multiply. Group leaders want their members to grow into full maturity in Christ. Multiplication indicates that is happening.

After all, what is the alternative to group multiplication? Imagine a group of eight members who meet weekly for years. Their group never grows because there are no new people won to the group, and no member ever grows to become a leader. That group is not making its maximum possible spiritual impact on its members or its community.

The goal of multiplying leaders is so central that it even shapes the way cell church leaders speak about their churches. Ask cell church leaders about the size of their congregation, and instead of giving you the number of members on the roll, or even weekend worship attendance figures, they will usually tell you the number of groups they have. Each cell has a leader, and leaders are making disciples who make disciples. The end goal of the church is developing disciples who make disciples, not attracting people to sit in the seats.

Defining "Disciple"

While it is important to emphasize that discipling others is part of "normal Christianity," it is not helpful or accurate to imply that those who are not leading cell groups are not disciples. "Disciple" simply means "learner," and any follower of Jesus is a disciple.

Joel Comiskey offers one way of viewing discipleship in progressive terms, as follows:

"D-1 disciple": one in a cell and the School of Discipleship learning the basics of the faith

"D-2 disciple": an apprentice leader, living out what he or she is learning and consciously preparing to be a cell leader

"D-3 disciple": a cell leader who has gathered some friends and family and is leading a cell group

"D-4 disciple": a multiplication leader; the leader has developed another disciple who is leading a cell group.[6]

What about Gift-Based Ministry?

How does the idea of every believer becoming a group leader square with the biblical teaching that the church is the Body of Christ, and that each member has a different function? (1 Corinthians 12). By seeking to make every member a group leader, are we trying to make everyone the same part of the Body? After all: "If they were all one part, where would the body be?" (1 Corinthians 12:19 NIV).

It is important to note that 1 Corinthians 12 is referring to spiritual gifts. However, as mentioned above, cell ministry is not a gift-based role; it is a maturity-based ministry. We can use our spiritual gifts in many different ways, but we do gift-based ministry in addition to the basic ministry of reaching others and discipling them.

Acts 6 is often cited as the beginning of role differentiation in the early church. Some widows were being neglected in the daily food distribution. To solve this problem, the apostles asked the church to select gifted individuals to oversee the food ministry, while the apostles continued to focus on prayer and teaching. Philip and Stephen were chosen for the task, and some today refer to them as the first "deacons."

It is important to note, however, that those first deacons were involved in evangelism and discipleship as well as food distribution. The Scriptures tell us that Stephen did miraculous signs and wonders among the people, and when he was arrested gave a penetrating public sermon to those who were about to kill him. After his selection, Philip also traveled to Samaria to preach the gospel and to minister to people. God used him as a witness to others; recall Philip's sharing his faith with the Ethiopian eunuch.

Philip and Stephen did not oversee food distribution *instead* of evangelism and discipleship, they did it *in addition to* that basic disciple-making function. In cell church terms, first they were group leaders; secondly they used their gifts to help the food distribution.

Although it is important for believers to identify and employ their spiritual gifts, using spiritual gifts should not be confused with spiritual maturity. The church at Corinth may have employed spiritual gifts more frequently than any other of the early churches. However, from Paul's letters, it appears they were the least mature of all his churches.

Further, we have no indication that Jesus selected his twelve disciples with an eye toward giftedness. In training them to make disciples of all nations, he did not say anything about using spiritual gifts. He simply

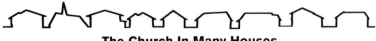

taught them to make disciples by preaching what he preached and doing what he did.

Christ-followers need not restrict their service to cell ministry. It is good for believers also to serve in specialized, gift-based ministry roles. Many Christians burn with God-given dreams and ministry passions. At the same time, if making disciples is part of "normal" Christianity, we cannot ignore it in favor of gift-based ministry. Would we say that because certain believers are singing for worship services that they are not required to love others? Since some count the offering and do the church accounting should they not be required to pray or to give? Let us build gift-based ministry on a platform of personal disciple-making.

Surprised by Ministry

Some of Crossroads' best group leaders have been those least convinced they could lead. When approached about becoming cell leaders, it is not unusual for people to respond, "I can't do that." Ironically, they are correct; at that moment they may not have the ability or maturity to help others grow spiritually. But that doesn't mean they could not be good group leaders! As they enter training they will grow and become equipped for ministry.

I don't know what mental picture Peter had of his future when he left his fishing boat and started following Jesus, but I'm pretty sure he didn't envision himself preaching a sermon that would produce three thousand converts, becoming a key leader for the dynamic early church, or dying as a martyr! If Jesus had told Peter all that he would end up doing, Peter might have said, "I can't do that!"

It is a good thing that Peter did not respond to Jesus' invitation by saying something like, "Jesus, I can't preach like you, but I am good with boats and fish. Here's an idea: You keep preaching, and I'll help the cause by forming a boat ministry! I can help with transportation, with feeding your team, and with financing your travel. I'll contribute fifteen percent of my fishing business income to underwrite your ministry. And when you are preaching to big crowds, I'll let you use my boats as a platform. In fact, I've got contacts all throughout this region. I'll set up a network of boats all along the shores of the Sea of Galilee. You do the preaching you're good at, and I'll do what I'm good at!"

That plan might sound reasonable, but the problem is that it is not what Jesus had in mind. Jesus told Peter, "Come follow me and I will make you fishers of people!" Then Jesus equipped Peter to do ministry Peter never

imagined he could do. After Peter's Pentecost sermon it was clear that Jesus had made Peter what originally he was not: a disciple who makes disciples. He does the same for his people today.

Mark was a member of my cell group. Though he was still fairly new at following Christ, after he had been in the group a while I sensed that he would soon be able to lead a group himself. One day I let him know I thought he would make a great group leader. He was unconvinced. He was quiet by nature, and had no ministry experience. Nevertheless, Mark entered the training process and has become a highly effective group leader. He has multiplied his group three times, and one of the groups he birthed has also multiplied. Recently he traveled with me on a trip to Europe, helping to teach about cell ministry. During one of his talks, through an interpreter, Mark said, "When I said 'Yes' to becoming a group leader, little did I realize that I would end up standing here in Budapest talking with you about group ministry!"

Jesus has a way of taking us to surprising places. When members say, "I could never share my faith, or pray for others," we need to share with them that Christ can equip them to do what they cannot naturally do themselves. We must not limit people's Christian service to areas of their natural strength. The Christian life is a supernatural one. We need to let people know that the Holy Spirit can empower them to do what they cannot do themselves.

Breaking the Church's "Glass Ceiling"

There comes a point at which believers hit a spiritual "glass ceiling." After growing rapidly as new believers, eventually they become restless or spiritually stagnant. At that point they might think that in order to grow deeper they need to learn some new truths, but, in fact, what they need to do is start passing on what they have learned. Whether they know it or not, no matter how much good teaching they hear, they will not grow significantly until they start helping someone else grow! Reaching out to others is an indispensable component of growing deeper in the faith.

Today, if people tell me they have been attending a cell group and they want to grow deeper, I say, "You are right, you need to keep growing. It's time for you to sign up for the School of Discipleship and get equipped to become a leader."

Identifying new leaders

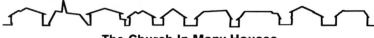

In order to grow larger, cell churches need more leaders. A church cannot have more cells than cell leaders. In order to grow deeper, believers need to become group leaders.

Cell leaders don't come ready-made; they must be developed. Cell churches develop members into group leaders by using a training process sometimes called the "equipping track" (which is discussed in the next chapter). As group members progress through this equipping process, they are taught to lead a group of their own. Leaders who disciple their members and multiply their groups are continually aware of how far each group member has gone in the equipping process. They don't try to develop new leaders all on their own. Instead, they encourage their members to take the next step in the equipping track. They know that while everyone can become a leader, some are closer to being ready than others.

When I look around my group for the person who will enter the equipping track and become the next leader, I am looking for potential rather than readiness to lead. I want to find someone who is ready to begin the development process. I look for a person with the following traits:

A growing relationship with Jesus Christ. Not spiritual perfection, but authentic growth and evidence of a changing life.

Faithfulness to the group. This person makes it a priority to regularly attend the group meetings, and follows through with any assigned ministry tasks.

Commitment to the vision of the church. Cell leaders have delegated pastoral authority, and therefore they significantly influence their group members. It is vital that they influence them in a way that is consistent with the philosophy and vision of the church. Someone who does not agree with the church's values cannot be a group leader.

Relational connection with other group members. Do others in the group respond to the potential leader?

When I find someone with the above potential, I seek to help that person take the next step in the equipping track. Sometimes they respond, "I'm not ready to be a leader." That may be true! But then, that is why we developed an equipping process! We don't wait for people to feel ready to lead; we want to help them become ready.

Realistically, not everyone in the church will become a group leader. At the same time, we will keep letting everyone know it is within his or her reach. Some who today don't think they can lead a cell will find themselves doing so tomorrow!

NOTES

1. Erwin McManus: *An Unstoppable Force* (Loveland, CO: Group Publishing, 2001), 31.

2. Ironically, using a gift of teaching usually hurts multiplication. The members might appreciate the leader's teaching, but most will say "I could never do what our leader does . . . I don't know nearly enough and I can't teach that way, either!" So they never step forward to lead.

3. Joel Comiskey, *Home Cell Group Explosion* (Houston, TX; Touch Publications, 1998), 26.

4. Ibid.

5. Henderson, *John Wesley's Class Meeting*, 101.

6. From an e-mail from Joel Comiskey.

CHAPTER SEVEN

Moving from Educating to Equipping

"On the whole, I do not find Christians, outside of the catacombs, sufficiently sensible of conditions. Does anyone have the foggiest idea what sort of power we so blithely invoke? Or, as I suspect, does no one believe a word of it? The churches are children playing on the floor with their chemistry sets, mixing up a batch of TNT to kill a Sunday morning."

"It is madness to wear ladies' straw hats and velvet hats to church; we should all be wearing crash helmets. Ushers should issue life preservers and signal flares; they should lash us to our pews. For the sleeping god may wake someday and take offense, or the waking god may draw us out to where we can never return."
—*Annie Dillard*

Tim had been inviting Marie to attend his cell group for quite some time. She had been worshiping at Crossroads for years, and although she had heard a lot about groups, she had never joined one. So, Tim was pleasantly surprised when Marie finally accepted his latest invitation to visit. During the meeting, Tim noticed that Marie participated comfortably and seemed to fit in easily. Tim was anxious to hear what she thought of her group experience, so he called her the next day.

"It was nice, Tim," Marie answered, "but I don't think it's for me. I want to go deeper in Bible study." Tim tried to explain to her the purpose of a small group and the teaching role of the School of Discipleship, but it didn't seem to make any difference to Marie. Tim was bumping into a conflict of assumptions: the difference between educating and equipping.

Discipleship and Equipping

For many Christians, discipleship is synonymous with education. As a result of this mindset, the classroom has become the center of discipleship in most churches. When people think of advancing spiritually they most often think of learning more about biblical and theological matters.

Cell churches view discipleship differently. Of course, they instruct believers and help them to learn. However, communicating information is not their main focus. Cell-based churches focus sharply on equipping all believers to evangelize and disciple others.

As a result, discipleship ministries in cell churches take on different forms than they do in non-cell churches. In many cell churches there are no Sunday schools, no pastor's midweek Bible studies, and few midweek worship services. Even the cell group itself is different in nature than the program-based church's "small group."

Not all cell churches are structured alike, but one trait they share is the goal of mobilizing each member to be a disciple who can make disciples. Cell churches seek to help each member adopt both the character of Christ (the Great Commandment), and the mission of Christ (the Great Commission). Their primary goal is to equip each member to reach and disciple unchurched people. By equipping each member to make disciples, the cell church can blossom into a movement that is able to penetrate a region with the gospel.

Jesus the Equipper

Jesus' public ministry was quite short. Amazingly, in just three years of ministry he literally changed the world. As we saw earlier, Jesus accomplished this by equipping twelve men to carry on his mission.

It is important to note *how* Jesus equipped these twelve disciples. Jesus did not say, "Meet me on the hill outside Capernaum every Tuesday evening from 7-9 p.m. Bring your scrolls, because I'm going to be teaching through Genesis verse by verse—then we'll move on to a discussion of Exodus, and then right into Leviticus." Jesus took a different approach. He said, "Come, be my disciple, and I will show you how to fish for people!" (Matthew 4:19 NLT). When embarking on his public ministry, Jesus didn't start a class; he gathered a small group! That small group was Jesus' chosen vehicle for accomplishing his purpose of equipping the Twelve to make disciples (or, as he said, to "fish for people").

Jesus' discipleship strategy was shaped by the knowledge that after a few brief years he would ascend to heaven and his mission would be left in the hands of the disciples he would train. So, for three years he focused on preparing the Twelve to carry out his mission. Had Jesus only

educated the Twelve about kingdom truths but had not equipped them to spread the gospel, there would be no Church today.

The Difference between Educating and Equipping

The process of learning to drive can illustrate the relationship between educating and equipping. When it came time for my three sons to get their driver's licenses, their first step was to enroll in Driver's Education class. In this helpful class they learned about the rules of the road. They also saw films about the dangers of reckless driving, were shown the location of select parts of a car, and heard lectures about what to do in various driving scenarios. In short, they were educated about driving a car, but they were not yet equipped to drive.

After completing the classroom instruction and passing the Department of Transportation's written test, my sons obtained learner's permits. This meant they could start to practice driving. Our state requires student drivers to log fifty hours behind the wheel while accompanied by a fully licensed driver (who is often a parent clutching the armrest).

Finally, after the required number of hours of practice driving, my boys were qualified to take their driver's license exams. At test time, the Department of Transportation did not care whether my sons had attended a Driver's Education class. Even if the boys could quote passages of the driver's manual by memory, it would not have helped them at this point. The examiners were concerned with only one issue: Are these young men able to safely operate a car according to the rules of the road? In order to earn their driver's licenses, my sons had to show they could translate the information they had learned in class into safe driving on the road. They had to demonstrate that they were equipped to handle a car responsibly. Then, and only then, did they receive their licenses.

People are educated when they know something. People are equipped when they can do something with their knowledge. Accumulating knowledge is part of the equipping process, but it is not the whole. Church leaders must not confuse the task of educating people about spiritual matters with the task of equipping them to change the world by making disciples.

As a pastor, I was trained primarily to educate people in classroom-centered programs. The very names of those programs revealed their academic orientation: "Sunday *School*," "Christian *Education*," "Bible *Study*." (For a number of years I even wore an academic gown while preaching.)

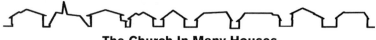
I had never stopped to consider questions like: For what purpose are the members in "school"? What exactly is the desired result of their Christian education? I suppose I assumed that if people learned enough about the Bible and were informed about what God expected, they would live out the faith with increasing dedication. In reality, I had been shaped more by the academic thrust of the Reformation era than the strategy of Jesus.

The Power of Equipping

What might happen if churches focused on equipping members to do more than serve in church programs? What if we went on to equip each of them to make disciples?

Ironically, one of the striking examples of the world-changing power of equipping people is the Communist party. For more than twenty years, Douglas Hyde was a dedicated member of the British Communist Party before he became a Christian and resigned in 1948. While news editor of the *London Daily Worker*, he was involved in recruiting and training leaders for the Communist movement. Years after his conversion, Hyde wrote a book titled *Dedication and Leadership*, which examined the Communist Party's training methods and what the church can learn from them.

In this book, Hyde does not set out to refute Communism's ideological fallacies. Instead, he describes how the Communist movement equipped its members to make an impact on the world. Hyde asserts that Communism could spread in a free nation like England because Communists focused on equipping every party member not only to understand Communist philosophy, but also *to actively advance it.*

The party employed a careful strategy in order to accomplish its goal of activating each member. It started with the beginner's orientation class. When newly recruited Communist Party members arrived at class expecting to learn why Communism was superior to Capitalism, they quickly discovered they were in for more than an intellectual exercise. Hyde writes:

> [The student] will first be made to feel right from the start of the very first session that instruction is not an end in itself; that acquiring knowledge may be interesting but that this should have some purpose. He is made to understand that the knowledge he gains will be so much ammunition for the fight, something to be used, not just absorbed. And he can see that this is not just words for all around him are people who are living the Communism he is being taught . . .[1]

This emphasis on acting on the party teachings also influenced the way the instructors taught. Hyde wrote, "Each tutor is expected as he prepares his notes to ask himself the question, 'education for what?'"[2] Communist theorist Friedrich Engels answered that question by saying, "The philosophers have only tried to explain the world, the job, however, is to change it . . ."[3]

While history has shown Communism to be a failed philosophy, we should not miss the point that the Communists' equipping process was designed to transform each party member into an active soldier in their struggle. With this strategy it is no wonder they influenced the twentieth century the way they did.

The church can learn much from Hyde's observations. The Communist party, even with its flawed foundations, made an impact the world by equipping each of its members to advance its cause. How much more can the church change the world through the power of the Holy Spirit by equipping its members? Christian leaders can agree with Engels' position that the goal is to change the world. Of course, Christ-followers have a different vision of the kind of change the world needs, but Jesus' example showed that the way to effect that change is to equip others to fulfill the mission. That can happen best when it is clear to every Christian believer (and teacher) that the information our churches teach is meant to be "ammunition" for the mission of reaching others for Christ.

Equipping and Spiritual Growth

As a pastor, I am always pleased to hear people say they want to grow spiritually. However, I have discovered that a great many Christians equate "going deeper" with acquiring new information. This is not necessarily an accurate equation.

Essentially, spiritual growth means becoming more like Jesus. Sadly, a person may be able to quote the Bible extensively or debate many fine points of theology, yet still remain mean-spirited, self-centered, and chained by sinful habits and hang-ups. The indicator of true spiritual growth is not an increased feeling of spirituality, nor attainment of a certain level of biblical knowledge. Spiritual growth produces an inner and outward transformation.

In the timeless Christian classic *Imitation of Christ*, Thomas á Kempis said:

> Indeed it is not learning that makes a man holy and just, but a virtuous life makes him pleasing to God. I would rather feel contrition

than know how to define it. For what would it profit us to know the whole Bible by heart and the principles of all the philosophers if we live without grace and the love of God?[4]

Equipping helps people grow spiritually because it requires applying the Scriptures. James 1:22 tells us, "Do not merely listen to the word, and so deceive yourselves. Do what it says" (NIV). Christians who put their biblical knowledge into practice will grow spiritually. Churches that create a culture of "just do it" will grow strong and vital Christ-followers. This verse says that hearing scriptural truth without acting on it amounts to an act of self-deception. Hearing without acting is spiritually harmful because it gives us a false illusion of growth. We think we are growing while we are really not! The Bible is meant to change the way we live.

Even though most cell churches do not have midweek Bible studies or Sunday School classes, they do not ignore the importance of the Scriptures. Rather, they create the opportunity to emphasize their application. When we teach people too often, the hearers frequently do not have enough time to grapple with the text and apply it to daily life. For example: If I am a dedicated member of a traditional church, I may hear quite a number of teachings. On Sunday morning I will hear the pastor preach the Scriptures, and as a result I am to change my life. Then I might attend a Sunday School class, at which I hear another passage taught. The message of that text is also meant to change my life. Suppose I also attend a midweek Bible study or service. Again, I hear a biblical teaching and I am challenged to apply it (which will change my life). Can I really be expected to change my life several different ways each week? Or are we being educated beyond our obedience?

Cell groups emphasize application. For example, instead of introducing new Bible study material in the midweek, most cell groups use questions based on the weekend sermon as their curriculum. This way, group members who listened to the sermon develop an application mindset, which prevents them from becoming inoculated against the power of the Scriptures.

Part of the reason the early Methodists were such a vital movement is they emphasized biblical application. D. Michael Henderson writes:

> The messages delivered within the Methodist system were exhortations to do something rather than make speeches about something. "Avoid speechifying altogether!" Wesley warned his preachers...The style of the Methodist preachers might be compared to that of the

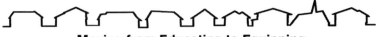
Greek orator Demosthenes, who was described as follows by one of his contemporaries:When his rivals speak, the audience applauds: "What a magnificent speech!" When Demosthenes speaks, the Athenians cry in unison, "Let us march on Philip!" Insipid sermonizing was studiously avoided, and whole generations of local and traveling preachers were schooled in the science of harnessing human motivations.[5]

Developing an Equipping Strategy

Equipping believers for ministry takes more than good intentions. It requires a strategy. While there is no such thing as *the* cell church method of equipping believers, it is safe to say that all effective cell churches employ some kind of defined "equipping track."[6] Each church designs its own approach, and methods are constantly evolving.

An equipping track is a set of clear steps designed to help a person grow from a new believer into a leader of group leaders (that is, a disciple who makes disciples). The track consists of both classroom teaching and personal mentoring.

For illustration purposes I will briefly describe the equipping process at Crossroads Church. This is just one of many possible approaches. We have drawn from elements common to many cell churches around the world, and made them our own. Those are:

1. Cell Group
2. Encounter Retreat
3. School of Discipleship/Leaders
4. Coaching Group

These components were briefly described in earlier chapters, but let us revisit them to see specifically how they contribute to the equipping process.

1. Emerging leaders start growing in the cell group.

The process of leadership development starts with the relational discipleship of a cell group. The purposes of the open cell group are: a) to help members grow spiritually by applying the Scriptures to their lives, and b) to reach the unreached. As members participate in these purposes, they grow more spiritually mature. When group members band together to reach out to their unchurched friends, they stretch their faith in new ways. They also develop an outreach mindset. As they discuss how to apply the Scriptures, they open their lives to God's work and develop a habit of obedience. In addition to helping members grow through community and application, the cell group also provides a supportive environment for apprentices to gain leadership experience.

To help facilitate biblical application, most cell churches (including Crossroads) provide their groups a set of questions based on the weekend sermon. These questions are prepared by the staff, and serve as the curriculum for the groups. The purpose of the questions is to stimulate application of the point made in the sermon. For example: After a sermon that highlights God's call for us to forgive others, the lesson might include questions such as:

- Share a time when you were forgiven.

- Whom do you sense God calling you to forgive more fully right now?

There are several benefits to using a sermon-based group curriculum, including:

a) *There is no teaching pressure placed on the group leader.*

A group leader is not a teacher. Since the pastor has already done the teaching during the weekend sermon, the group leader merely facilitates as the group members discuss how to apply it. This means the group leaders need not have the gift of teaching, and therefore more people can be group leaders.

b) *Using sermon-based questions promotes worship attendance.*

Though members can still participate meaningfully in the group if they did not hear the weekend message, the link between the lesson and the sermon naturally encourages the members to be present at worship.

c) *Each lesson is self-contained.*

A new person can feel awkward about joining a group that is halfway through a twenty-four-week study book. By contrast, discussion questions prepared from the sermon will not presume prior experience or knowledge. Furthermore, the life-based questions allow the group to be oriented toward people, not curriculum.

d) The lessons are application-oriented.

This helps the members develop the habit of putting the Scriptures into action. It promotes true-life change, and provides a built-in support and accountability group for each group member. The cell group is about application of the Scriptures in a relational context.

Apprenticeship: On-the-job equipping

Another important component of the equipping process that takes place in the cell is apprenticeship. Soon after agreeing to start leadership training, a group member will start to share the ministry tasks with the group leader. The cell leader provides on-the-job training by asking the apprentice to lead portions of the group meeting or to do some between-meeting ministry work. The leader then provides feedback so that the apprentice learns how to do everything the leader does. The newly emerging leader is called an "apprentice" instead of an "assistant" in order to communicate that this person is a trainee and not just a helper.

2. Emerging leaders are motivated and prepared by the Encounter Retreat.

Once people have been participating in a cell group, their leader encourages them to attend an Encounter Retreat. The International Charismatic Mission (ICM), a huge cell church in Bogotá, Colombia, developed this retreat. ICM noticed that many Christians were hampered in their spiritual growth and service by hang-ups and habits they had acquired through the years. The Encounter Retreat is designed to help people break free from the hurts and guilt of their past by experiencing God's love and grace. In many ways, the Encounter is a variation of the popular Walk to Emmaus or Cursillo retreats. (Although at Crossroads, the Encounter Retreat is twenty-eight hours long, instead of seventy-two hours like the Walk to Emmaus).

Crossroads Church has adapted the Encounter Retreat to provide experiential ways for people to realize they are new creations in Christ. Each time we hold an Encounter we see people overwhelmed by the grace and love of God. The participants are deeply moved because of the Encounter's atmosphere of unconditional love and the focus on the cross of Christ. Time after time we see that when participants return home they start to mend relationships, change habits, and recommit themselves to

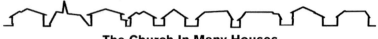

spiritual growth. The more broken our society becomes, the more this kind of ministry will be necessary.

The Encounter is not an isolated spiritual enrichment event offered by the church. Instead, it is part of the larger strategy of leadership development. At the end of the weekend the spiritually renewed participants are challenged to use their newfound freedom to serve others. They are challenged to enroll in the School of Discipleship and train to become a cell leader.

3. Emerging leaders are taught in the School of Discipleship.

Also known as the School of Leaders[7], the School of Discipleship is a series of classes designed to help equip group members to become group leaders. It is information with a purpose. Students will not move from one level to the next simply by showing up for classes. They are expected to act on what they know before moving on to the next level.

At Crossroads Church, the School consists of three levels, each one thirteen weeks long. Each level has a prerequisite and an action step attached to it. They also include quizzes to ensure the students understand the information. The classes are offered on Sunday mornings so they do not compete with group meetings. We consistently have resisted compressing or shortening the levels into less than thirteen weeks because it takes time to develop leaders. The School is designed for brand-new believers to become equipped as leaders. In order to gain the necessary experience and spiritual maturity the students need more than the School's information; they also need time in the cell. One cannot microwave strong leaders.

Level One teaches basics of the Christian faith. To be eligible for Level One, the students must be members of a cell group. In addition to participating in the class, the students are challenged to invite two people to their small group by the end of the term. This is important because a leader who is unwilling to invite new people will create a stagnant group.

Level Two is for those who are serving as apprentices in their groups. There are two sections to this class: a survey of the Bible, and techniques of group leadership. At the conclusion of Level Two the students are encouraged to start a group.

Once members are leading a group they are eligible to attend Level Three. Here they receive spiritual enrichment designed for those who are in group ministry. They will also be instructed on the basics of how to mentor and coach other group leaders. They will need those mentoring skills when their group multiplies and they start coaching the new leaders.

The School of Leaders does not presume to teach believers everything they will ever need to know about the faith, the Scriptures, or ministry. Much of their leadership development will come from their experiences in a group and their relationships with other leaders. However, the school does give people enough training so that they can begin to take the first steps into ministry. It is important to clearly define the steps into ministry. Otherwise, many believers will assume they are unqualified to lead.

The School defines the core knowledge required to start leading a group. It does not provide enough information to equip them to be a Bible teacher, but that is not the goal. The School, in conjunction with a cell group, will equip believers to start leading a small group. Once they are leading they will have the opportunity to learn more as they feel the need to do so.

4. Coaching Group: Discipling the Leaders.

The Coaching Group continues equipping leaders in the context of personal relationships. As explained earlier, group leaders participate in two kinds of groups: they lead an open cell group and they also participate in a coaching group comprised of fellow leaders. Long after group leaders have completed the basic equipping of the School of Discipleship, they continue to learn and grow. They meet regularly (at Crossroads it is at least twice per month) with their coaches, where they receive personal mentoring and instruction. Sometimes they will meet individually with their coach, at which time they can deal with personal spiritual and leadership issues. At other times coaches meet in a group setting with all the leaders they mentor. This allows leaders to receive valuable input and encouragement from their peers. The coaches may also take that opportunity to teach a brief spiritual growth lesson to the leaders.

Ongoing Equipping

In addition to the School of Discipleship, cell churches frequently offer other equipping opportunities, such as:

a) Leadership Rally

At this monthly gathering of all group leaders, a staff (usually senior) pastor recasts the vision of the church, and encourages

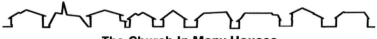

the group leaders through teaching and worship.

b) Advanced Equipping

After completing the three levels of the School of Discipleship and launching and multiplying their groups, leaders can attend optional short-term classes. However, these classes are open only to those who are actively involved in the vision of the ministry. We do not want to encourage people to "sit and soak," but if people are using what they are taught to minister to others, we will teach them as much as they can absorb!

c) School of Teachers

Some leaders who are gifted in teaching will want to go on to teach in the Encounter Retreat and the Schools. They can be equipped to do so through special training at a School of Teachers.

An Equipping Track

1. *Cell*: Application of Scripture

2. *Encounter Retreat:* Personal preparation for growth

3. *School of Discipleship:* Foundational teaching and training

4. *Coaching Group:* Life-based discipleship and mentoring

5. *Advanced Equipping:* On-going teaching/Bible study

There are many other equipping methods being used by cell churches around the world. There is no such thing as the ideal equipping track. As Joel Comiskey and M. Scott Boren write:

Many churches assume the magic lies in the equipping model. They can simply visit a church, copy its equipping curriculum, and immediately disciple their people. But there's no magic in the curriculum. Most churches pass through multiple revisions of their equipping track before finding the right fit.[8]

Crossroads' process, described above, will probably be modified in the future as we discover new needs and methods. There can be many answers, but the inescapable question for every church is: How will we equip leaders?

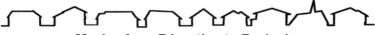

What about "Deep Teaching"?

Because cell churches do not offer adult Sunday School or midweek Bible studies, some might suggest that they do not offer substantive teaching. However, a careful analysis of this equipping process will reveal that there is no shortage of solid teaching in a cell church. Does the cell church offer instruction in the basics of the faith? Yes, (in School of Discipleship Level 1). Does it offer systematic study of the Bible? Yes, (in Advanced Equipping Level). Does it teach life-based discipleship principles? Yes, (in cell group and leadership group).

The main difference between the cell and the non-cell church approach to teaching lies in the fact that in the cell church a member cannot opt out of leading a group and still participate in Bible study classes. The cell church offers classes only for those who are (or who are preparing to become) group leaders. This approach helps to prevent members from adopting a "sit-and-soak" mentality. It also sends the message that helping others grow (as a group leader) is an indispensable part of normal Christian development.

Sum of the Parts

Early in Crossroads' group development history we made the mistake of expecting the small groups to accomplish too much. We thought the groups would be able to evangelize new people and completely provide for all the discipleship needs of believers. We expected the on-the-job training of an apprenticeship to be the only training new leaders would need. We soon learned differently.

One of the reasons for the effectiveness of the equipping process described above is the impact of specialized function. Each component of the discipleship track has a distinct purpose and function. The function of the open cell group is to reach out to pre-Christians while providing care and basic spiritual growth for Christians. The purpose of the Encounter is to provide readiness and motivation for group leadership to be trained. The purpose of the School of Discipleship is instruction for group leadership. The Coaching Group provides ongoing personalized discipleship and care to group leaders. No single component is expected to provide all that is necessary for spiritual maturity, but taken as a whole, all the pieces work together to equip the believer for maturity and ministry.

Again, the early Methodist movement provides a historical model. The Methodists used specialization in their spiritual growth strategy.

Henderson writes:

> One strategy which greatly enhanced the success of the Methodist system was the clear focus in each instructional mode on only one type of objective. Wesley avoided the temptation to try to accomplish too many purposes in any level of instruction. He carefully kept the various functions of his movement separate by limiting each group level to one major function: class meetings to alter behavior, societies to present information, bands to perfect "affections", and so on.[9]

Let us not settle for an educated church membership. Let us equip believers and mobilize them to fulfill the mission of Jesus.

NOTES

1. Douglas Hyde, *Dedication and Leadership* (Notre Dame, IN: University of Notre Dame Press, 1966), 49-50.

2. Ibid., 74.

3. Ibid., 51.

4. *Imitation of Christ*; Thomas á Kempis; Chapter 1 "Imitating Christ and Despising All Vanities on Earth" (From CCEL.org website).

5. Henderson, *John Wesley's Class Meeting*, 154.

6. Sometimes the word "equipping" is used to describe leadership development, whereas "discipleship" refers to the process of spiritual growth. However, it is not necessary to draw a distinction between them. In fact, each concept assumes the other.

7. Some churches use the term "School of Leaders". We have chosen the term "School of Discipleship so that those who don't consider themselves "leadership types" will not disqualify themselves before they experience it. Plus, the term communicates that helping others grow is a normal part of discipleship.

8. M. Scott Boren, and others, *Making Cell Groups Work Navigation Guide* (Houston, TX: Cell Group Resources, 2003), 423.

9. Henderson, *John Wesley's Class Meeting*, 145.

CHAPTER EIGHT

Moving from
Programs to Relationships

"Disciple making is not a program but a relationship."
—*Greg Ogden, from* Transforming Discipleship.

"And all the believers met together constantly and shared everything they had."
—*Acts 2:44, NLT.*

The Grand Canyon is one of the most awe-inspiring natural wonders of the United States. Those who visit it say its sheer size and scope of colors cannot be fully captured by a picture. Why does the Grand Canyon look like it does? What forces shaped it? Most likely it was the power of the Colorado River, perhaps with the help of a glacier, which carved out that beautiful sight.

If you turn a telescope toward the moon on a clear night, you will get a good look at the craters that dot its surface. Why does the moon's surface look like it does? Astronomers tell us that asteroids slamming into the surface and leaving craters shaped its distinctive look.

While natural forces shape natural features, people are shaped by other people. For example, my parents never gave me formal English lessons. I speak English because I grew up around them and picked up the language they spoke. Whether it is "doing the wave" at a ball game or wearing the latest fashion, the people around us shape much of our behavior and thinking.

The Bible reveals that God wants to shape us into the image of Jesus. One of the primary means God uses to reshape our lives is Christ-centered relationship. As author and denominational leader Reggie McNeal says, "God sculpts our souls through friends in our lives." [1]

I can attest to the truth of McNeal's assertion. Looking back over twenty-five years of following Christ, the most significant influences in my spiritual life have been people I can still name. I think of my high school friend

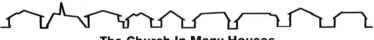

Richard, who invited me to his youth fellowship, where one of the leaders later challenged me to follow Christ. I think of the Christian guys I lived with in college, and how their values, habits, and perspectives rubbed off on me. I think of fellow seminary students whose dedication and maturity influenced me. My life has been deeply shaped by the relationships I have enjoyed with other Christ-followers.

"It's all in who you know" can be a complaint about biased hiring practices. But it can also sum up a spiritual truth! Just about everything God wants to do in and through your life will involve relating to another person. Authors Henry Cloud and John Townsend say, "People are God's 'Plan A.'" In their outstanding book *How People Grow*, they write:

> Biblical growth is designed to include people as God's instruments. To be truly biblical as well as truly effective, the growth process must include the Body of Christ. Without the Body the process is neither totally biblical nor orthodox.[2]

When we choose to invest in Christ-centered relationships, we are choosing to become more like Christ. On the other hand, if we want to make sure God doesn't alter the status quo of our lives, all we need to do is maintain a safe relational distance from other believers.

A Relationship-Based Church

Since people shape people, a church that seeks to stimulate genuine spiritual growth in its members must catalyze authentic, Christ-centered relationships.

Jesus demonstrated that relationships are essential to the disciple-making process. Mark 3:14 tells us, "[Jesus] appointed twelve—designating them apostles—that *they might be with him* and that he might send them out to preach" (NIV, emphasis author's). Jesus got personal with those he sought to develop. When he wanted to transform people deeply, he issued the invitation to "come follow me" (Matthew 4:19; Luke 18:22).

The modern church has largely replaced this relational focus with programmatic activity. Tragically, churches can be very lonely places for far too many people. Even while actively involved in church programs, countless men and women are living with quiet desperation and secret hurts known to no one else. We cannot hope to truly disciple people into Jesus' image if we leave them in their isolation.

Cell churches are essentially relationship-based churches, and cell groups are the greenhouse in which authentic relationships grow. By placing

groups at the center of their ministry, cell churches create an opportunity for their members to move beyond superficial contact and into true Christ-centered community.

Developing a Relationship-Based Church

A church does not become relationship-centered simply by offering small groups. Any congregation that wants to promote Christ-centered relationships needs to take practical steps to protect that relational focus from the forces of church life and daily routine which can easily swamp it. The following are some of the common ways cell churches assure that authentic relationships remain at the core of the church.

Eliminate programs

This idea may be hard for leaders of program-based churches to swallow, but it is almost a mantra in cell-based churches.

Open the weekly bulletin of most large program-based churches and you will see a flurry of activities listed. Whether it is ministry to young mothers, hospital visitation training, midweek classes, committee meetings, the building is buzzing with activity seven days a week.

While most churches seek to offer as many programs as possible, cell churches do not. Cell-based churches grow by multiplying cell groups, not by multiplying programs and events. Pick up a bulletin from a cell church and you will see very few, if any, programs listed. With no Sunday school, men's breakfast programs, or women's ministry meetings, the calendar of a cell church might seem downright empty. For example, Bethany World Prayer Center, a cell church in Baton Rouge, Louisiana, with an attendance of over ten thousand, boasts no programs at all. But a lack of programs does not indicate a lack of ministry. Cell churches carry out their ministry through holistic cells instead of through programs. Cell groups are not programs; they are the basic expression of the church. The life of the Body of Christ is found in the cells.

An inherent conflict

When I first heard that cell churches eliminate most programs, I dismissed the idea as unrealistic. I thought, why not embrace "the genius of the *and*"; that is, do cell ministry *and* offer other programs? I was soon to find out why cell churches avoid programs.

When we first launched cell ministry, we got off to a strong start. Enthusiasm was high among the group leaders. The groups were growing and multiplying rapidly. Our vision was clear; our efforts were focused.

Then I dreamed up what I thought was a great ministry idea: Our church could throw a huge "pre-evangelism" party for our area! We'd call this day-long festival "Septemberfest," and our members could invite their unchurched friends. Our hope was that after enjoying the food, booths, and music, our unchurched friends would be more open to an invitation to attend worship at Crossroads.

Septemberfest was a huge undertaking, requiring us to mobilize many teams of volunteers. The congregation responded wonderfully, and the festival was terrific. The event went off without a hitch and was lots of fun. Most members brought guests, and over one thousand people enjoyed the day.

But a funny thing happened along the way. I noticed that in the months preceding Septemberfest, our group attendance dropped. Some groups temporarily stopped meeting. Our group leaders and members had become so busy preparing for the festival that they didn't have time for their groups. We had thrown a great party, but we had lost momentum in our group ministry, and it would take us months to regain it.

Since then I have come to realize that there is an inherent conflict between programs and cell ministry. In the final analysis, we did not see a significant increase in first-time guests to worship following Septemberfest. Instead of spending hundreds and thousands of hours producing that program, what if our members had invested that time in building their small groups? I am convinced that the long-term fruit would have been greater and more lasting.

A matter of time

Local church ministry is lived out in daily realities. One of those realities is that church members have a limited amount of time. That means churches must prioritize their efforts. By limiting the number of programs it offers, a church can focus members' time on what is most important. Given the choice between having our members spend a Tuesday night forming friendships with pre-Christians at a barbeque, or spending it attending a church committee meeting, I would choose the barbeque in a heartbeat. If one has to choose either a heart-to-heart conversation with a fellow believer about their struggle to forgive, or making centerpieces for the church Valentine dinner, it would not be a hard call.

For a long time I wanted to say, "Maybe people can do both." But the reality is that every program we call our people to support means there is that much less time for them to be engaged in relational evangelism and discipleship.

A cell group is essentially a set of relationships. Cell ministry takes time because developing relationships take time. Cell groups are built when a leader and a member go out for coffee, or when a member invites a pre-Christian to hit golf balls. It takes time to call a fellow member and follow up with a prayer request. One cannot microwave a relationship. If church members are busy attending committee meetings, helping out with the midweek children's choir, and teaching midweek classes, they will not have the time needed to build a cell group. If the cell group is the best place to fulfill the functions of the church, then it does not make sense to allow anything else to compete with it.

Early in our transition to the cell model, our staff caught a glimpse of how freeing it can be to focus exclusively on cell groups. We were guests at Cypress Creek Church in Wimberley, Texas, which is a dynamic cell-based congregation of more than one hundred cell groups and a worship attendance of one thousand. As part of our visit, we sat in on their weekly staff gathering. The meeting lasted an hour and a half, and over one hour of that time was spent in worship and prayer. They spent only twenty-five minutes on "business" (I timed it!). Without dozens of programs to administer, the main agenda was to stay spiritually energized, and for the senior pastor to nurture the staff so they could effectively lead other group leaders. It was a big contrast to our three-hour weekly staff meetings at Crossroads, which were crammed with decisions made necessary by our programs. We saw that a sharp focus on cells not only could be effective, but enjoyable!

Even though the world's largest cell-based churches do not have programs, some churches may still feel they need to offer some programs while building cell groups. In that case, the basic principle here is: group first. Do not let anything compete with the cell for top priority.

Promote cells over service

Early in our church's history, if a member of the church came up with a ministry idea and could gather a team of folks to accomplish it, we simply said "Great! Do it!" But today, when people approach us with program ideas, we most often decline them. Unless a ministry provides a step

toward cell ministry, we are not interested. We want to focus our time on what matters most. We do not discourage people from serving as greeters, or music team members, or any other ministry team. We simply say that if people need to choose one or the other, we hope they always will choose the cell group.

One way to emphasize the centrality of cells is to make them the subject of most communication. Announcements and appeals reveal the values of a church. If each week the church announcements center on the need for workers in various ministries, then people understand that service is valued highly. But if each week people hear an invitation to join a group or a sermon illustration about cell groups, then they pick up the idea that cells are where the action is.

Emphasizing cell groups over programmatic activity does not limit members to sitting in living rooms, however. After all, the cell is more than a meeting; it is a web of relationships through which the purposes of the church are accomplished. When we see the cell as the church, we realize that many activities that are done through programs can be accomplished even better in cell groups. For example, a church that wants to do outreach through "servant evangelism" (small acts of kindness done in Jesus' name) does not need to set up a separate program to do so. Instead, it can encourage and resource the cell groups to organize their own servant evangelism projects. This has several advantages. Those members who are not in a cell can join in with a group in an outreach. In the process, they can get to know the group members better, and perhaps join the group after the project is done. It also develops more leaders. When a church runs a program, one leader may mobilize one hundred people to serve. But if the ministry is done through ten cells, ten leaders may mobilize ten people each. This makes leadership more accessible (not everyone can mobilize one hundred people) and ten times more leaders get developed! Even large-scale ministry can be accomplished by pooling a number of groups together.

Cultivate transparency

A small group will not become a true community just because members spend time together in a living room. It is quite possible for people to pull their chairs close to one another while keeping their souls hidden from one another. Unless the members allow one another to see what is going on in their hearts and lives, they will remain at a relational distance.

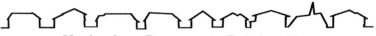
At Crossroads, we have sought to foster a culture of openness and honesty in several ways. The sermon illustrations often speak of both victories and defeats, revealing the humanity of the speaker. During worship we feature personal testimonies that do not shy away from sharing real life brokenness (as well as healing). The weekly cell group questions regularly invite participants to share honestly about the needs and events in their lives. Also, the Encounter Retreat involves a high level of transparency, and that often carries over into the life of the church.

Provide pastoral care through cell groups

Members of healthy cell groups care for one another. When cell members go to the hospital, it is not the pastor that cares for them—it is the cell. When cell members lean on one another during crisis, and express care for one another in times of illness, they become like a family. There is nothing like walking through deep waters with someone to forge a deep relational bond. At Crossroads' NewComers Class we inform the new attenders that the first line of pastoral care is the cell, not the pastor.

Confirmed by Research

One of the main reasons I was hesitant to shift to the cell model was that I wondered, *"Would the cell group be enough?"* Could Americans really be satisfied with only cell groups and no programs? It is well known that we Americans like choices and that many growing churches offer something for everyone. I wondered if cell and celebration would be enough to attract and hold people.

Today there is more than anecdotal evidence that cell ministry is enough. Recent research by Natural Church Development[3] shows that not only does cell ministry work, it works better than program-based approaches! Natural Church Development (NCD) pioneered a widely used tool for objectively measuring individual church health. The tool measures the eight essential quality characteristics of a church: leadership, gift-oriented ministry, passionate spirituality, functional structures, inspiring worship services, holistic small groups, need-oriented evangelism, and loving relationships.

NCD research in churches around the world affirms the principles of the cell church. First, it shows that small group ministry is the most vital ministry for a growing church. Specifically, "Our research . . . has shown that continuous multiplication of small groups is a universal church growth principle."[4] And,

"If we were to identify any *one* principle as the 'most important' . . . then without a doubt it would be the multiplication of small groups."[5]

After years of analyzing churches, in 2002 NCD turned its attention to cell-based churches to see how they compared with others. Its research indicates that cell churches are healthier and faster growing than non-cell-based churches. Note the following:

> . . . a study comparing the NCD scores of cell churches and non-cell churches showed that *cell churches overall scored significantly higher in all areas than non-cell churches.* [emphasis author's] Combined cell churches' scores averaged 59 while combined non-cell churches' scores averaged 45. Not surprisingly, Inspiring Worship showed the smallest difference (8 points higher for cell churches) and Holistic Small Groups showed the most difference (25 points higher for cell churches). Significantly, even churches that say they would focus on small groups over large group worship still had better scores for large group worship. This finding indicates that cells don't detract from corporate worship—they add to it.

> Additionally, the rate of church planting—in spite of the fact that the cell church movement has seemed to focus on getting larger rather than on planting more churches—would seem to indicate that multiplication is in fact in the genetic code. Cell churches averaged 2.5 churches planted compared to 1.9 churches planted for non-cell churches.

> Finally, the study showed that cell churches demonstrated an average growth rate almost double that of non-cell churches.[6]

Objective research now demonstrates that cell ministry produces growth in both quality and quantity.

What about Spiritual Gifts?

A program-based church is built on the spiritual gifts of the congregation's members. In order to offer a menu of ministry programs, a church must motivate many members to contribute their expertise and giftedness. But if a church has few programs, what is the role of spiritual gifts? After all, the Bible clearly teaches that we should know about spiritual gifts and that we should use them (1 Corinthians 12:1).

Even though they don't have programs, cell churches utilize the spiritual gifts of their people. They do so in both the small group and the larger church context.

Some of the important biblical passages that deal with spiritual gifts seem to assume they will be used in a small group setting. For example, 1 Corinthians 14:26 says, "When you come together, each one has a hymn, a lesson, a revelation, a tongue, or an interpretation. Let all things be done for building up" (NRSV). The words "each one" seem to indicate that the gifts were not used in a large group context, but in a smaller, house church setting. (How long would it take for each one in a gathering of five hundred people to bring a hymn?)

Someone with the gift of encouragement can frequently use that gift in a cell group. Members with the gift of administration will be of great help to a cell planning a social event. Those with the gift of teaching can utilize that in their group, too. An added benefit to exercising spiritual gifts in a small group setting is that one's giftedness level need not be as high as it might have to be if one were to use it in a large group setting. A person may not be gifted enough to teach a group of several hundred, but he or she could be a great help to a small group.

Members of cell churches can also use their gifts in a larger church context. Once they are in a group and moving toward leadership, members can also serve in various ministries as they feel led. At Crossroads Church we are pleased when a cell member steps up and serves on a ministry team. However, our main goal is not to get new people involved in the ministry team. Our primary goal is to help people connect to a cell group. They can serve in addition to, not instead of, growing spiritually in a group. If people are evangelized and discipled in cell groups, then every member can be on the front lines of the church's mission.

Be the Church

It used to bother me that there were few Bible verses that could be construed as commanding believers to "go to church." I felt that it was important for Christians to be present at the weekly worship service, and I was fairly sure that God felt the same way, too (even though it wasn't easy for me to prove it!). Today I believe that part of the reason I could not drum up more verses about attending worship is that during New Testament times a church's life did not rise or fall on a weekly event. Followers of Jesus were part of a new community that lived out each day in relationship with God and each other. Indeed, these churches were centered mostly in homes.[7] Yes, corporate worship was a significant part of their experience, but it sprang out of their life together. Church was not an event to attend; it was a community to which one belonged. It is no coincidence that we do not see many "go to church" verses. On the other hand, we can find many passages urging us to *be* the church: "Love one another," "encourage one another," "build one another up," etc.

By making cell groups the center of its ministry, the cell church leverages the power of relationship.

When we invest time in developing relationships with both believers and preChristians, we focus our attention on what is most important in ministry. The relational nature of cell groups is consistent with the relational nature of the church itself. This makes sense, because the cell group is the most basic expression of the Church. So when we focus on building relationships we focus on making disciples and building the church.

NOTES

1. Reggie McNeal, *A Work of Heart* (San Francisco, CA: Jossey-Bass, 2000), 127.
2. Henry Cloud and John Townsend, How People Grow (Grand Rapids, MI: Zondervan, 2001),122.
3. Natural Church Development International: Diedersbueller Str. 6 25924 Emelsbuell, Germanyinstitute@ncdinternational.org or www.ncd-international.org.
4. Christian Schwartz, Natural Church Development (Emmelsbuell, Germany: U.S.A edition: C & P Verlags, 1996), 32.
5. Ibid., 33.
6. From Joel Comiskey e-mail entitled "Cell Churches and the NCD survey," Coach Net:
   The Cell Church Chronicles, October 2002, email newsletter. I received this newsletter in my mailbox on October 21, 2002. I talked with Jeannette Buller, Bob Logan's key person, and she said that this study originated in Germany from the Natural Church Development database and was conducted by Christian Schwarz's key statistical person.
   For further information, write CoachNet@CoachNet.org.
7. For example: Colossians 4:15, "Give my greetings to the brothers at Laodicea, and to Nympha and the church in her house." Or, Romans 16:5, "Greet also the church that meets at their house."

CHAPTER NINE

Moving from Church with Cells to Church that is Cells

"The Bible does not prescribe any particular pattern of church organization. But today's practical necessities suggest the need for small groups as basic church structure—as always when the church has been at its best."

—Howard Snyder[1]

"The churches in the province of Asia send you greetings. Aquila and Priscilla greet you warmly in the Lord, and so does the church that meets at their house."

—1 Corinthians 16:19, NIV.

If aliens were to try to determine what "church" is by listening to people's routine conversations, they would end up very confused, because we use the word in so many ways. For example, we say that we:

- go to church
- construct a church
- attend church
- belong to a church.

So, what is the church? Is the church a building to enter, or an organization to which we belong? Or is it an event to attend? The way we answer that question deeply influences the way we do ministry.

In his book *Church Planting Movements*, researcher David Garrison documents the astonishing multiplication of churches in various parts of the world where spiritual renewal is occurring. In northern India, for example, four thousand churches were planted in ten years.[2] How is it possible for that many churches to spring up in such a short time? These churches are not brick buildings with steeples; they are house churches. They may not match a Westerner's mental image of church, but these small groups of people are fully functioning churches, effectively evangelizing and discipling their communities. As a result, they are multiplying at an amazing rate.

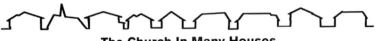

Though the cell church differs in some important ways from a house church, the common element is the small group nature of ministry. As mentioned earlier, the cell is the fundamental expression of the church. Just as the basic unit of life in a physical body is the cell, the basic unit of the Church (the Body of Christ) is the cell group. Indeed, in the cell church, the cell is not just a part of the church; it *is* the church.

When people tell me they want to visit our church, they generally ask for our worship times. While I am always glad to welcome them to worship, I often want to add, "If you really want to check out the church, you'll also need to see a cell group in action!"

The Cell Group as the Church

The cell group as church is not so much a philosophy to be implemented as a reality to be recognized. Church history documents that during times of ease and prosperity, the Church can take on a variety of forms. However, when the church experiences the intense stress of persecution, it is stripped away of anything superfluous, and it reverts to its most basic components. Governments may arrest its pastors, but the church is not the pastors. The authorities may confiscate its buildings, but the church is not the building. Hostile forces can outlaw public services, but the church is more than public worship. Historically, when persecution has driven the church underground, the church has taken the form of cell groups. By doing so it becomes very effective and resilient.

The Meserete Church of Ethiopia was a small, one-hundred-year-old evangelical denomination when the nation's government changed. In 1982 the Communists gained power and the church was driven underground. Leaders were arrested and church buildings were confiscated. Public worship became illegal. When the government fell ten years later and the church was able to emerge from underground, they discovered they had grown from five thousand to fifty thousand people.[3] After decades of little or no growth, suddenly their buildings could not contain the crowds coming to worship.

How did the Meserete Church manage not only to survive, but also thrive under persecution? They began to meet in cell groups. Even though they are now worshiping freely, they continue to do cell ministry because they have seen its effectiveness. One leader said, "Before, we used to pray for more people to come fill our benches. Now, we pray for more benches to handle all the people."

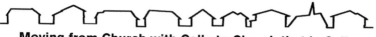

A similar story is unfolding in China, only on a far larger scale. When the Communists expelled all missionaries in 1950, many worried that the church in China would disappear. At that time there were approximately one million Protestants in the entire country. But instead of dying away, the church has exploded. Today, there are an estimated eighty million Christians in China. The vast majority of these are in unofficial house churches.[4] The cell group is the basic unit of the church because it can fulfill all the purposes of the church.

A Purpose-Driven Cell Church

In his book, *The Purpose-Driven Church*, Rick Warren identifies the five purposes of the Church as follows:

1. Ministry (Service)
2. Fellowship
3. Evangelism
4. Discipleship
5. Worship[5]

Warren maintains that in order to be healthy, a church must give appropriate attention to each of these five purposes. If we accept these as the core purposes of the church, the question becomes, what is the best way to fulfill these purposes?

Traditionally, churches assume that the answer to that question is to establish programs that focus on each purpose. For example, if a congregation felt the need to increase the "fellowship" quotient among its members, it could assign a staff person or lay leadership team to create programs that target this basic need. Those leaders would design a variety of activities, which would promote fellowship. They might set up a spot for coffee and donuts after the worship service. They could sponsor church-wide fellowship dinners, or church sports leagues, or fellowship groups, or any number of other programs. In this way, they hope to increase the level of fellowship among their members, and thus make the church healthier. By taking the same approach with the other four purposes of the church, a congregation can develop a well-rounded ministry. So the church becomes purpose-driven and program-based. That is, the congregation accomplishes the purposes of the church by creating and sustaining ministry programs. Practically, this means the staff members will spend most of their time administering the programs, and church members are urged to attend and volunteer with the programs.

The cell-based church is also purpose driven, but it fulfills those purposes differently. Instead of establishing programs, cell churches fulfill the purposes of the church through cell groups. In other words, the answer to most ministry questions is, "the cell group." For example, how will church members find meaningful connection (fellowship) with other believers? In a cell group. How can evangelism happen best? Through a cell group. How will people be discipled and grow spiritually? Through a holistic cell group (that is, a group which fulfills all the purposes of the church).

The reason that cell groups are the answer to most ministry questions is that the purposes of the church are accomplished best through relationships. Evangelism happens best in relationship because it is easier to lead someone to Christ if we know the person than if we do not. (Over eighty percent of believers were brought to faith by the influence of a family member or friend.) The best discipleship is relational discipleship because God uses the people in our lives to shape us into the image of Jesus. By definition, fellowship requires personal relationship. And ministry, or service, is the releasing of people to serve other people. The purposes of the church are fulfilled in the context of relationship. And we cannot know a large number of people personally; we can only know a small group of people well.

Therefore, cell groups are not just one way to fulfill purposes of the church; they are the best way. With the exception of worship, which may be fulfilled best when the corporate body of the church assembles on a weekend, the cell group is the best way to accomplish the functions of a healthy church. [6] Program-based churches tend to see their small groups as a way to fulfill just one or two of the church's purposes. A cell church looks upon the cell group as the primary way to accomplish all the purposes of the church (with the possible exception of worship). This is why some cell churches can grow so large without an elaborate system of programs. Each cell group carries all the "DNA" (purposes) of the church. By replicating holistic cells, the church grows.

Some of the house churches that are multiplying so rapidly in China have been dubbed as POUCH churches. They are named that because of the characteristics they display:

Participative Bible study and worship

Obedience to God's word as the mark of success for every believer and church

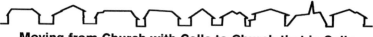

Unpaid and multiple church leaders

Cell groups of believers meeting in

Homes or storefronts.[7]

Though cells are not house churches, the characteristics of a POUCH church also describe healthy, holistic cell groups and churches.

Why It Matters

Viewing the cell as the church is far more than a theoretical abstraction, it profoundly influences the decisions and priorities of church life. Just a few of the ways the impact shows up include:

- *Church membership*—If the cell is the church, can someone be a member of a local church without belonging to a cell group? If so, what exactly is he or she joining?

- *Ministers*—Lay/clergy distinctions tend to dissolve when the cell is viewed as the church, because the leader takes on a kind of pastoral role. That is, the leaders care for the needs of group members with delegated authority from the pastoral staff. This influences the selection, training, and supervision of group leaders.

- *Resource allocation*—Funding and facility decisions are made with the goal of strengthening the cell groups.

- *Staff time*—Effectiveness for staff people is measured in terms of the health and multiplication of groups, not attendance at programs.

- *Church health measures*—Most churches measure their health by the number of people attending the weekend worship experience. If the cell is the basic unit of the church, then analyzing church health starts with the number and the vitality of the cells.

Cell group ministry is truly a New Testament model. It was not unusual for the Apostle Paul to conclude his letters by referring to the church in someone's house. For example:

The churches in the province of Asia send you greetings. Aquila and Priscilla greet you warmly in the Lord, and so does the church that meets at their house (1 Corinthians 16:19 NIV).

Greet also the church that meets at their house (Romans 16:5 NIV).

Give my greetings to the brothers at Laodicea, and to Nympha and the church in her house (Colossians 4:15 NIV).

Obviously, these groups were not large. But Paul named these small groups of Christians as full-fledged churches! Those same principles of the New Testament church have an impact on the world today.

Your neighbors may not realize that the small band of believers that pulls up in your driveway each week is actually the church. It is fine if they still think of your congregation as the church on the corner of 5th and Washington. But you will know better. You will know that your congregation is the Church in many houses.

NOTES

1. Howard A. Snyder, *Radical Renewal; the Problem of Wineskins Today* (Houston, TX: TOUCH Publications, 1996).
2. David Garrison, *Church Planting Movements* (Midlothian, VA: WIGTake Resources, 2004).
3. This story is documented in the video *Against Great Odds*; by Gateway Films.
4. David Aikman, *Jesus in Beijing* (Washington D.C.: Regnery Publishing.), 7.
5. Rick Warren, *The Purpose Driven Church* (Grand Rapids, MI: Zondervan, 1995).
6. Many cell churches include worship in their cell group meetings. However, they still worship as a corporate body on the weekends.
7. Garrison, *Church Planting*, 62.

Part III
Strategic Issues

CHAPTER TEN

First Steps

"Just because we don't know how to do something doesn't mean we shouldn't try to do it."

—Reggie McNeal

Transitioning to a cell model requires wisdom, tact, and Spirit-led timing. One simply cannot stand up one Sunday morning and announce that the church is going to become cell-based.

So how does one go about leading a program-based church to become a cell church? There is no single answer to that question. Just like the answer to the question, "How do I get to Main Street?", it all depends on where you are starting. The transition of a one-hundred-and-fifty-year-old traditional church will look different than that of a nine-year-old meta-church congregation. However, there are some steps that are universally applicable. This chapter offers some suggestions on where to start when transitioning to a cell-based church, and answers to some common questions about implementing a cell-based ministry.

Getting Started

The senior pastor must lead the way

We must start with the senior pastor's role because the cell church cannot function without the senior pastor's complete commitment. In a program-based church a volunteer or staff member can be designated as Small Groups Coordinator. But in a cell church the senior pastor is the chief cell pastor and the primary cheerleader. Cell ministry must be shared by all, but primary leadership cannot be delegated to another staff person.

When lay people ask me how they can get cell ministry started, I tell them that without the involvement and support of the senior pastor they will not be able to sustain a meaningful cell ministry. This is not to downplay the importance of the laity or other staff. It is simply to recognize that if indeed cell ministry is the foundation of the church and not just a program, the senior pastor must be in the center of the action. A senior pas-

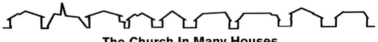

tor can take initial steps toward cell ministry without the complete support of the congregation, but the reverse is not true.

As a lay person, you can talk with (not pressure!) your pastor about cell ministry, and pray that God will lead. If you are a staff person or a lay person, you might consider giving this book to your senior pastor.

If you are a senior pastor who is interested in transitioning to cell ministry, I would encourage you first to take sufficient time to retool and reorient yourself to the cell ministry paradigm. Before you do anything else, catch a clear vision of cell ministry and the role of the senior pastor in a cell church. This usually involves reading, praying, and visiting.

Read All You Can

Because the philosophical foundations of the cell church are quite different than that of the program-based churches, it is vital to read a lot. It takes more than one book to truly absorb the theology, methodology, and values of the cell church. (You might start with the books listed in the Resources section.)

There are many good seminars, conferences, and books available. Network with other cell pastors and leaders and tap their experience.

As you read, bore in on how cells reach and disciple people. Identify the priorities of cell ministry. Understand how an integrated cell system works in a local church. What would it look like if that were lived out in your setting? What part does a senior pastor play in coaching and leading other leaders? Can you see yourself doing that? Are you willing to stay long enough to birth it in your church?

Pray for God's Will

As you learn more about the cell church, pray and ask if this is the direction God wants you to go. It is vital to settle this matter in your soul, because at some point in the transition your resolution will be tested. You will need the conviction that cell ministry is God's call both on your life and for the church you serve. Pray until you know.

Visit Other Cell Churches

In many ways, cell ministry is more caught than taught. By spending some time in a functioning cell church environment, you will pick up cell ministry values.

Attitude Adjustments

When transitioning to cell ministry, one of the most important attitude shifts senior pastors need to make is that of changing their focus from the large group to the small group. Most pastors measure the vitality of the church by the number of people attending the Sunday morning worship experience (the large group). Therefore, much of a pastor's time and attention is given to attracting people to the celebration service.

But cell church pastors evaluate church health in terms of group development and multiplication. Therefore, they focus time, money, and staffing on growing cells. They may know the weekend worship service attendance figure, but they also can tell you how many people were at cell groups the week before. They realize that if the number of healthy cells grows, the worship attendance will grow, too.

Again, we can learn from the early Methodists. They were vitally concerned with the development of their groups (classes), therefore ministers were urged to focus on the health and growth of class leaders. In his book, *Class Leaders*, David Lowes Watson quotes the observations of Thomas Coke and Francis Asbury, which were printed in the 1798 edition of the *Doctrines and Discipline of the Methodist Episcopal Church in America*. The following remarks were titled "Concerning Class Leaders":

> The office is of vast consequence. The revival of the work of God does perhaps depend as much upon the whole body of leaders, as it does upon the whole body of preachers. For our leaders under God are the sinews of our society, and our revivals will ever, in a great measure, rise or fall with them.

Since the health of the church depends on the vitality and effectiveness of the group leaders, developing leaders becomes a high priority for cell church pastors. Senior pastors who are transitioning to the cell model will find their schedules increasingly filled with visits with cell leaders, strategizing about cell ministry, and training future leaders. Indeed, the most strategic time cell church pastors spend is that which is given to the development of cell leaders. Adopting this people-oriented mindset is an essential ingredient of effective cell ministry, and anything we can do to promote it is helpful. When the cell-based Cypress Creek Church in Wimberley, Texas built their beautiful new worship facility, they intentionally included no offices for pastoral staff. They wanted their pastors to be out discipling people, not holed up in offices working on church programs.

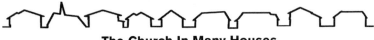

Start One Group

Once the cell vision burns in your spirit, you sense God's leading, and you have a good understanding of how a cell church works, it is time to start a group.

As senior pastor, you do not need official board action or a congregational vote in order to begin cell ministry; just start a cell! Start small; don't try to launch a dozen groups at once. If you do, you probably will not be able to train and coach leaders adequately, and the cells will not stay healthy. Build the ministry on the firm foundation of well-equipped leaders who have experienced healthy cell ministry. Launch slowly and think long term. Start one cell, equip a new leader, and then multiply that cell into two groups. Coach the new leader and repeat the process for each group. The power of multiplication will expand your ministry in a sustainable way.

Suggestions for starting a group:

1) Choose a format.

As the initial group leader, the senior pastor decides on the proposed group's agenda and curriculum. Will the group format be based on the "4 Ws" (see chapter two)? Will it use Bible study questions based on the Sunday sermon, or something else? (Since members will be inviting unchurched people to the group, it is important that the material require no prior biblical knowledge, and that it not require a visitor to have attended a previous meeting in order to participate.) As senior pastor it is important to remember that you are setting the template for future groups, so be sure to choose a format that can and should be replicated.

2) Make a list of people you wish to invite.

Pray about whom God would have you invite to become part of your first group. It is not necessary to start with the established leaders of the church (though it is fine to do so if they are open to the idea). You can also look to those at the edges of the congregation and to those newest to the church. Seek those who are teachable and want to grow. You could even invite some unchurched persons. It can also be helpful to include a few people who are already close to being ready to lead a group themselves, though that can be hard to discern ahead of time.

3) Pray for the people on the list for two weeks.

Ask God to make the people on your list receptive to your invitation.

4) Invite the people on your list to the first meeting.

Don't start with too many people; five to seven people will be about right. If the group gets too large too quickly it will be difficult to foster true intimacy and community. Starting with a manageable number of people will allow you time to train a new leader to help with the group as it expands.

Make your first meeting light and enjoyable. Share a meal, host a game night, or enjoy some other interactive activity. At the end of the event, share the vision of the cell and invite people back for the following week.

It is important to lead the first cell to operate exactly as you want future groups to function. Emphasize and model outreach right from the beginning; do not allow it to be a closed group under the guise of training future leaders. People will reproduce what they experience.

As they lead the group, pastors need to realize that they are setting the precedent for what future group leaders will be and do. Therefore, lead as you expect future leaders to lead. For example, during group discussions, cell members may be inclined to ask the pastor for the "right" answers to any biblical or theological questions. Resist the temptation to provide those answers. As a pastor, if you teach or become the resident theological expert, you will find it hard to develop another leader because the group members will think, "I can't lead a group like Pastor does. I don't have the theological education."

5) Focus on leadership development

One of the skills cell church pastors need is the ability to equip and mentor others. In a cell church, effective senior pastors develop new group leaders and, later, coach those who will coach leaders.

As soon as your first group is up and running, start to think through how you will train and care for emerging leaders. In the early phases, when you have only one or two leaders, you may not need to use the formal structures of something like a School of Discipleship. The training track can be much more personalized.

In Crossroads' early days, when we had only a few groups, the leaders met with me in a living room every other week for training, prayer, spiritual growth, brainstorming, and evaluation. We had no formalized equipping track, but we learned together in "real time."

Adopt a "mentoring mindset." As soon as your first group begins, start looking for the group member who is most ready to be developed into a cell leader. Share various group ministry tasks with that person (and provide encouraging feedback). Let that person see who you are outside of the group meeting. Cast vision and pray with that emerging leader. As you gradually release more ministry responsibility to the apprentice, the rest of the group will view the apprentice as a leader. At that point you can set a date to birth the group and become the new leader's coach.

Dealing with Resistance

As the early groups are quietly growing and multiplying the senior pastor can be training and casting cell vision to the church board and other leaders. However, even those leaders who approach the transition process with great love and patience can find that the shift to a cell-based philosophy may eventually evoke some conflict. After all, most major changes within churches do. I do not know if it is possible to avoid losing any members in the transition (every pastor hopes so!), but here are a few suggestions for minimizing friction:

Consistently teach cell church values (the concepts in chapters four through nine). Before making structural changes, seek to influence the values of the congregation. As people adopt cell church values, implementing cell church forms and structures eventually will seem natural.

Publicly share stories of the life change that is happening in the groups.

Approach structural changes slowly and carefully. Let established programs continue while adding cell ministry components.

Show love to all, whether they embrace the cell vision or not.

Transitioning a church to the cell church paradigm is a very big undertaking, and we have space in this chapter only to scratch the surface. Each church's journey will be unique, yet God guides committed leaders through the whitewater rapids of change.

CHAPTER ELEVEN

Frequently Asked Questions

Putting cell church principles into practice can produce many questions about details. Here are some of the more common ones.

Q: I'm trying to start cell ministry, but the members of our church don't seem interested in getting into a group. What can I do?

Remember, you are not trying to reorganize the congregation into groups, so do not feel you need to recruit the pillars of the church into groups. It is not necessary and it probably will not even work. Your existing members are probably satisfied with their spiritual growth and their relational network at the church. After all, that is why they are still there!

When starting the first cells, invite everybody, but focus on growing your groups from new people, not necessarily the core members. Pastor Larry Stockstill said, "We consistently focus our attention on new converts and visitors: the 'growing edge' of the church where the least resistance to relationships is found. Gradually, many of the 'late adopters' have seen the benefits of a cell relationship and are becoming involved. Now about sixty-five percent of the congregation attends a cell each week."[1]

Q: How can we be sure the group leaders will not drift into wrong teaching or a different vision?

Realistically, we cannot be sure it will never happen. However, when leaders are trained, developed, and adequately coached, they will rarely become divisive or "loose cannons." The School of Discipleship helps shape the values of emerging leaders as they repeatedly hear the vision of the church. Leaders also submit regular reports that allow the church staff to get a sense of what is happening in each group.

Isolation produces problems, so make sure every cell leader also has a coach through the "Jethro structure"(see chapter two). If a leader is resistant to accountability, that will show up quickly and that attitude can be addressed. Group leaders who will not be accountable or teachable will lose the privilege of leading.

Q: Won't we be breaking up friendships by asking the groups to multiply?

No. Instead of losing friends, group members will expand their circle of relationships. After a group birth some of the members might not see one another at group meetings as often, but their friendships will remain, and they will make new friends in the new groups as well.

When group members express resistance to multiplying the group, they need to be reminded that a group with no new members will become stagnant and eventually die. So if they want to maintain the level of community they are enjoying, they need to offer it to others.

We also continually need to remind group members that the purpose of the group is to evangelize and disciple others. In short, it is not all about them. Sometimes sacrifice is called for in order to accomplish God's mission.

A couple of practical tips: It is best not to refer to a group as "splitting"; it is always "birthing" (a much more positive image!). Also, do not attempt to assign people to a group. When it is time to birth, the members choose whether to go with the new group or stay with the original. Neither is it wise to link the birthing of a group to a specific attendance number (for example, "When the group gets to twelve people it must birth.") That can actually discourage people from inviting others to the group.

Q: Where do leaders and coaches find the time for all those meetings?

Cell ministry does take time. However, if there are few other church-related time demands, and if the get-togethers are uplifting and add value, members will see them as gatherings they look forward to instead of meetings they are obligated to attend.

If the relationships between group leaders and coaches are strong and healthy, they will actually look forward to getting together because it means spending time with friends. When coaches and leaders get together, they need not always discuss a cell group issue, either. They may simply build their relationship by getting together for dinner or going to a ball game.

Q: What if someone asks: "The School of Discipleship classes sound interesting. I never intend to lead a cell group, but can I enroll anyway?"

The School of Discipleship/Leaders is not a Sunday school class or Bible

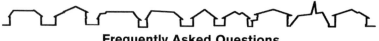

study for general learning. It is designed to equip group leaders. Perhaps some day the person will want to lead a group, but the School is only for those moving on toward group leadership.

Q: If there are no other programs and the School is only for those preparing to lead, what educational opportunities does the church offer those who don't want to become leaders?

Those who do not want to lead a group can participate in the life of the church in almost every way. Of course, all are welcome at the worship services, and anyone can attend a cell group or the Encounter Retreat. It is important that everyone in the church feel loved and valued, whether they lead a group or not. No one should ever feel forced to become a leader. While everyone has the opportunity to become more fully equipped and to lead a group, no one should ever feel forced to do so. For some, it is simply not the right time to step more deeply into ministry.

However, cell churches generally do not offer classes and Bible studies apart from the equipping track. They invest in equipping the members who want to move into ministry. That makes real the principle that discipling others is "normal Christianity."

Q: What is the role of the board and church committees in a cell church?

The role of the Board evolves as the church transitions to the cell model. When cell ministry is in an embryonic stage, the role of the board is much different than when it is mature. When cell ministry is fully implemented, the structure of the church becomes quite simple.

A delegation visiting Crossroads from another church asked me, "In light of your cell group emphasis, what does your education committee do?" I said we do not have an education committee, because the cells and School of Discipleship take care of educating and equipping people for ministry.

Another visitor asked, "If you do not have any committees, who will do the work around the church?" When there are few programs, there is little programmatic work to do, and therefore few committees are required! The work of the church is done through the cells.

In keeping with our church's polity, we do have three or four standing committees at Crossroads (Pastor-Parish Relations, Trustees, Nominations) The role of the board will always be important. At the same time, ministry is not centered in committee meetings; the real action is in the

person-to-person ministry of the cell.

Changing church administrative structure is not the first step in transitioning to a cell philosophy, but change will be required. As the church evolves into further cell maturity, keep trying to simplify as much as possible and resist adding more structure or programs.

Q: How does cell ministry affect church staff roles?

The role of a staff person in a North American cell church is generally "cells, plus something." That means staff persons know that their first job is to multiply cells and to coach leaders. This makes every staff member a "small groups pastor." However, most churches will also add additional responsibility to the staff role (communications, administration, missions, etc.).

Cell churches focus staff time and attention on developing cell leaders. Again, Wesley took this approach centuries ago. D. Michael Henderson noted that in Wesley's Methodist movement, the primary function of leadership was to equip others to lead and minister, not to perform the ministry personally. "Rather than performing the 'ministry' themselves, the leaders' main task was the training or equipping of the leaders at lower levels."[2]

Not only do staff persons focus on growing groups, cell church staff often emerge from the groups. Kevin started attending Crossroads Church and then joined a group. He quickly became an apprentice, then a leader. He multiplied his group and started coaching other leaders. Eventually he was invited on staff at Crossroads before leaving to plant a church in another state.

It is encouraging for members to know that if they sense God's leading, they can become a staff person by multiplying so many groups that we need to pay them to coach them all!

Q: Can our Sunday school classes function as cell groups?

Sunday school classes are fundamentally different in nature than cells.

By definition the cell meets outside the church and has a strong evangelistic goal. Sunday school classes are instruction-based, and meet inside a church building.

The environment of a home is much different than the institutional feel of a church facility. In a healthy cell, members encounter life together, sharing experiences outside the group. A classroom environment produces a classroom culture. It is highly likely that in spite of the Sunday school class' intent to become a cell group, if they meet at Sunday school time in a Sunday school room they will revert to being a Sunday school class instead of a true cell group.

Also, the School of Discipleship works best when offered on a Sunday morning since it doesn't require people to commit to another evening out. It is not strategically advantageous to set up a scheduling conflict between cell group and School of Discipleship.

On a practical note, cell ministry is less expensive than Sunday school, because cell groups utilize homes instead of classrooms that will only be used a few hours per week. It may not be wise to suddenly cancel a long-standing Sunday School program at the beginning of a transition to cell ministry, but be conscious of what receives publicity and nurture.

Q: How do you minister to children in a cell-based church?

Cell churches vary widely in their approach to children's ministry. Some will offer a children's church experience and then fold children into intergenerational cell groups. Other churches choose to have children meet in cells in homes with an adult leader.

At Crossroads we currently offer a "cell and celebration" experience for children at the church facility during worship hours. Divided into age-appropriate groups, first the children participate in large group experiences. They sing, hear a story, watch a video, or experience some other form of creative communication. Then they break up into small groups with an adult and talk about the Bible story for a few minutes.

Even though it incorporates a small group component, our children's ministry actually functions as a program. We have found it to be the best approach for us, but each church makes its own choices in this area.

Q: What about youth ministry?

Student ministry can be cell-based because students can lead cells!

At Crossroads the senior high is entirely cell-based and operates on the same format as the adult ministry, although they have their own equipping track. Because younger students are not always ready to lead by themselves, the middle school (grades 6-8) is partially cell-based. They meet weekly at the church (a non-cell idea) for the large group gathering, but also in cells. Some groups are led by middle school students, others by adults. In many ways the middle school ministry is a transition stage between the programmatic children's ministry and the cell-based high school ministry.

Q: How can we help new worship attenders get into a cell group?

The best way for people to get into a group is through a personal invitation. No announcement from the front will ever be as effective as a face-to-face conversation between two friends. So, teach group leaders to be actively inviting new worship attenders to visit cells at weekend services.

Also, the new members class can be leveraged for group recruitment. During the class, talk about the role of groups in the church's life. Tell stories. Let new attenders know that pastoral care happens in groups, so if they want a sense of belonging and the chance to receive the best personal care, they need to be in a group. Use small group break-out sessions to give them a taste of talking with others.

Make group ministry visible at the weekend services through sermon illustrations and through the testimonies of the members. Make sure attenders know whom to talk with or what to sign so they may express their willingness to try a group.

Q: What about social outreach in a cell church?

Amidst the focus on evangelism and discipleship, some may wonder if social action and ministry to the poor have a place in the cell church. The answer is, "Yes." Indeed, a strong cell system can foster motivation to serve those in need.

The early Methodist movement is a good example of this dynamic. Methodist Church founder John Wesley was highly focused on evangelism. At one point he declared that Methodists have "nothing to do but to save souls." Yet for all its evangelistic zeal and small group focus, the Methodist movement was also characterized by great social concern. Wesley and the early Methodists provided people in need with education, medical care, prison ministry, and more. The class meetings (group ministry) produced committed, servant-hearted believers who were spiritually vital enough to reach out.

Spiritual growth and works of mercy are not mutually exclusive. When believers participate in a healthy cell group, their spiritual growth fuels their desire to meet the needs of others. Indeed, if our soul is not vitally linked to Christ through spiritual growth, the desire for social action can eventually fade (or at least become distorted). Works of mercy alone are not enough to feed the soul. Writer Evan Howard observes:

> Interest in spirituality has hit mainline Christianity like a flood. Our experience with social justice has led us to see that outer change without inner change has little staying power and often leads to burnout for those devoting themselves to kingdom work. We are ready for a good dose of inner spiritual transformation.[3]

One who is in vital, growing relationship with Jesus is going to serve others with increasing passion and purity. To try to do works of mercy without this relationship invites not only burnout, but also a loss of our bearings as we try to bring about God's kingdom by human efforts.

Cell churches can mobilize believers for works of service, usually without creating large programs to do so. For larger projects, several groups can band together in order to make a bigger impact. For example, a couple of Crossroads' men's groups joined together to offer free oil changes for single moms in our area. Other groups take donated items to nursing homes. Other groups lent aid to a family that lost their home in a fire. Crossroads also sponsors national and international short-term mission trips. We find that the majority of those who respond to these challenges are part of cell groups.

NOTES

1. Quoted in Joel Comiskey *Home Cell Group Explosion*, 71.

2. D. Michael Henderson, *John Wesley's Class Meeting* (Nappanee, IN: Evangel Publishing House. 1997), 138.

3. Howard Evan, "Three Temptations of Spiritual Formation"; *Christianity Today*, Dec. 9, 2002 Vol. 46 No. 13.

CHAPTER TWELVE

Only the Spirit Gives Life

"The answer won't come from another seminar . . . We have too many mere technicians who are only stressing methodology, and they are increasingly invading the church. Then answer is not in any human methodology. The answer is in the power of the Holy Spirit. The answer is in the grace of God."[1]

—*Jim Cymbala*

"Not that we are competent in ourselves to claim anything for ourselves, but our competence comes from God. He has made us competent as ministers of a new covenant—not of the letter but of the Spirit; for the letter kills, but the Spirit gives life."

—*2 Corinthians 3:5-6, NIV*

In order to understand the incredible growth and vitality of huge cell churches around the world, we need to look beyond philosophy and structure.

As important as it is to understand the philosophical shifts needed for cell church ministry to work, the key to building a vital congregation of any sort does not lie in organization alone.

Lawrence Khong, who pastors a dynamic cell church in Singapore, reminds us, "The structure of the cell church is nothing but a conduit for the power of the Holy Spirit. Unless the living water flows, our churches are dead, our cells are useless, and our lives are powerless."[2]

"Will the cell church model work here?" It is a valid question to study and explore. At the same time, let us remember that it is not a system which "works"; it is God who works through yielded people. No ministry model will change lives without God's power.

In an earlier chapter the church was compared to a furnace. Though some units are more efficient than others, it is not really the machinery of the furnace that keeps us warm. It is the flame that burns inside it which produces the heat!

To focus exclusively on cell structure and philosophy is to build the fireplace without starting the fire. A spiritually dead church does not spring

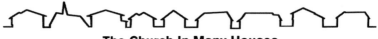
to life simply because it is organized as a cell church. It really doesn't matter if you have cell groups that are spiritually dormant. We can't rearrange a bunch of dead wood and expect to get warm. We need the fire!

While we build the conduit of cell church structures, it is vital to seek God's power to fill the forms. Some of the ways we can open our ministries to God's Spirit are through prevailing prayer, depending on God, and inviting Christ's presence.

Prevailing Prayer

Acts 2 tells us that the Church was born in a prayer meeting. The disciples were gathered in prayer, just as they had been for weeks, when the Holy Spirit came upon them on the day of Pentecost. Would the Spirit have fallen on them if they had been playing volleyball instead of praying?

Extraordinary prayer is one of the common denominators in cell churches worldwide. International Charismatic Mission in Bogotá and the huge churches in Korea hold daily early morning prayer meetings. Members gather at the church building as early as 5 a.m. in order to ask for God to work among them.

For the last five years, I have had two pictures hanging prominently behind my desk. One was taken inside the sanctuary of Yoido Full Gospel during prayer time. It is the image of fifteen thousand people standing with raised hands as they prayed aloud to God. The other picture hangs a few inches below it. It is picture of me bowed in prayer alone in a prayer closet at the Kwang Lim Methodist Church's Prayer Mountain retreat. I keep these pictures prominently displayed as a visible reminder that if I want to see the crowds won to Christ, I must spend time alone with God; if I want to see the church pray, I need to pray myself.

Each church finds its own way of coming together in prayer. At Crossroads we have not emphasized early morning prayer. Instead, we have engaged in corporate prayer during First Wednesday leadership rallies. We have convened special "Concerts of Prayer." We also have held individual prayer vigils. Even so, we still have much to learn and a long way to go. How will your church reach out to God in corporate prayer?

Depending on God

Only the Spirit of God can do the work of God. If we are going to make a lasting difference, we need to stay in vital union with Christ. In John 15:5 Jesus said, "I am the vine, you are the branches. Those who abide in me and I in them bear much fruit, because apart from me you can do nothing" (NRSV).

No doubt all of us would nod our assent to the importance of this verse. But the depth of our belief in its truth shows up in our schedules and actions. I have learned that whenever my energy and attention to structural issues rises higher than my attention to matters of the spirit and the heart, I have crossed over into self-reliance. At that point I have slipped into trying to build the church for God by my own effort.

Pastors and cell leaders who learn this lesson are blessed indeed. Mark, one of our cell leaders, e-mailed me after he experienced this truth in a vivid way:

> My new small group has turned into a large group. [A couple of weeks ago I started with five in my group] Can you believe that I had fifteen people there last night, including myself? I had been praying that God would work in the hearts of the people I invited and bring them to the group and he has done so in abundance. It's an incredible blessing and I am really fired up by it. But fifteen is a lot and I'm wondering what my next step should be. Fortunately, Floyd is apprenticing (another blessing) so he is able to jump in and lead part of the group. I've already started praying for guidance on this . . .

> I can't even begin to express what an incredible experience this has been. I am so thankful for and humbled by the way God has brought this together. The really interesting thing is that I really wasn't content with the way the group's first meeting went and I realized that perhaps I wasn't depending on God enough to do the work. So I started to focus strictly on that. The last two meetings have been fantastic.

As we develop our group leader training material, let us remember to teach our leaders how to depend on God for practical needs.

Christ's Presence in the Cell

It was one of those group meetings. There was no energy in the room. The members were discouraged, even depressed. Some were battling fears and guilt. A few did not even want others to know they were attending the meeting.

Then something unexplainable occurred: a supernatural presence invaded that room. At that moment, not only did the meeting dynamics change, so did its members! When the meeting started they had been listless and despondent, but when they left they were enthusiastic, faith-filled, and determined.

The group meeting I am referring to is recorded in the book of John chapter 20. Jesus had been executed, and his disciples were wondering if they would be next to be arrested. Then:

> On the evening of that first day of the week, when the disciples were together, with the doors locked for fear of the Jews, Jesus came and stood among them and said, "Peace be with you!" After he said this, he showed them his hands and side. The disciples were overjoyed when they saw the Lord.
>
> Again Jesus said, "Peace be with you! As the Father has sent me, I am sending you." And with that he breathed on them and said, "Receive the Holy Spirit. If you forgive anyone his sins, they are forgiven; if you do not forgive them, they are not forgiven."
>
> Now Thomas (called Didymus), one of the Twelve, was not with the disciples when Jesus came. So the other disciples told him, "We have seen the Lord!"
>
> But he said to them, "Unless I see the nail marks in his hands and put my finger where the nails were, and put my hand into his side, I will not believe it."
>
> A week later his disciples were in the house again, and Thomas was with them. Though the doors were locked, Jesus came and stood among them and said, "Peace be with you!" Then he said to Thomas, "Put your finger here; see my hands. Reach out your hand and put it into my side. Stop doubting and believe."
>
> Thomas said to him, "My Lord and my God!" (John 20:19-28 NIV).

This was a hinge event for those disciples. When the risen Jesus entered the room, everything changed.

The most attractive part of a cell meeting is not the Bible application discussion or even the sharing of our personal stories; it is the presence of Christ. When people experience the nearness of the risen Lord in our cell meetings, we will not have to cajole them into attending the following week. Christ's presence will accomplish more than we can imagine.

Each group meeting needs a vertical dimension. Warm fellowship and community are important, but not enough. For a cell group to be truly alive, it needs a sense of the holy so that when group members walk away at the end of the night they feel that they have been in the presence of God.

Of course, we know that Christ will be present whenever we gather. After all, he promised, "For where two or three come together in my name, there am I with them" (Matthew 18:20 NIV). Although Christ will be present, we need to welcome him. Two ways to open the door of the group to God's presence are worship and prayer.

Worship draws group members' attention heavenward and introduces the vertical dimension to a cell meeting. It can be very meaningful to sing God's praises in a cell group, especially if someone knows how to play guitar or piano. However, some group members can become self-conscious about singing in a cell gathering. There are other ways to worship, though, such as:

- reading a psalm of praise aloud together then pausing in silence
- getting on one's knees to pray aloud together
- quietly listening to a song from a worship CD.

The key objective is to glorify God and help the members connect their hearts to the presence of God.

Prayer also ushers us into God's presence. When leaders arrive at the meeting having already prayed for the Spirit to work in that night's gathering, the members will be more likely to experience God. As group members share personal needs, the best response is not advice or even empathy, but prayer. Not only will prayer help the people at that moment, but when their requests are answered it creates the realization that "God is at work among us!"

One of our leaders wrote to me:

Last night my small group had communion . . . We all brought food to share. We went around and talked about how God has blessed us this year. I could not believe what people were saying about the group. Here are just a few comments I heard as we went around the circle:

"I only thought I could find 100 percent acceptance at my twelve-step program, until I came to this group."

"I have been a Christian for years, but this group has helped me grow in my faith and ask myself questions about God that I have not thought of before."

"I have found peace for the first time in many years. My children and I are not exchanging gifts this year, but focusing on Christ and just spending time with one another."

"It's not that my children are perfect now, it's that God has changed me and so I look at situations differently."

[The leader went on to share an incredible answer to prayer, and a touching story about the healing of a relationship.]

We served one another Communion, and it was so powerful. You could feel the presence of the Holy Spirit as if you could reach out and touch him.

I have been so busy lately. It just slowed me down and helped me focus on what is really important. I cannot believe the change in these women and how much the support of this group means to them. God is working in the hearts of these women!! It was one of those moments that renews my commitment to small group leadership.

God is using ordinary people each day in extraordinary ways through cell ministry. It really is possible to change the world by making disciples who make disciples!

NOTES

1. Jim Cymbala, *Fresh Power* (Grand Rapids, MI: Zondervan, 1991), 14. Quoted in Making Cell Groups Work.
2. Lawrence Khong, *The Apostolic Cell Church* (Touch Ministries International, 2000), 99.

Resources

Suggested Reading:

Astin, Howard. *Body and Cell.* new updated ed. Monarch Books: London, 2002.

Bandy, Thomas C. *Christian Chaos.* Abingdon Press: Nashville, Tennessee. 2001.

Beckham, William. *The Second Reformation.* Touch Publications: Houston, Texas. 1995.

Boren, Scott. *Making Cell Groups Work.* Touch Publications: Houston, Texas. 2002.

Boren, Scott, Comiskey, Neighbour, and Beckham. *Making Cell Groups Work.* Touch Publications: Houston, Texas. 2002.

Navigation Guide. Touch Publications: Houston, Texas. 2003.

Cho, Dr. Paul Yonggi. *Successful Home Cell Groups.* Logos International: Plainfield, New Jersey. 1981.

Coleman, Robert Emerson. *Master Plan of Evangelism.* Revell, Fleming H. Co.: Ada, Michigan. 1994.

Comiskey, Joel. *Cell Church Solutions.* CCS Publishing: Moreno Valley, California. 2005.

Comiskey, Joel. *Home Cell Group Explosion.* Touch Publications: Houston, Texas. 1998.

Comiskey, Joel. *How to be a Great Cell Group Coach.* Touch Publications: Houston, Texas. 2003.

Comiskey, Joel. *How to Lead a Great Cell Meeting.* Touch Publications: Houston, Texas. 2001.

Comiskey, Joel. *Leadership Explosion.* Touch Publications: Houston, Texas. 2000.

Comiskey, Joel. *Persistence and Passion.* Touch Publications: Houston, Texas. 2004.

Comiskey, Joel. *Reap the Harvest.* Touch Publications: Houston, Texas. 1999.

Finnell, David. *Life in His Body.* Touch Publications: Houston, Texas. 1995.

Galloway, Dale. *20/20 Vision.* Scott Publishing: Portland, Oregon. 1990.

George, Carl. *Prepare Your Church for the Future.* Revell, Fleming H. Co.: Ada, Michigan. 1991.

Green, Michael, editor. *Church Without Walls.* Paternoster Press: Waynesboro, Georgia. 2002.

Hornsby, Billy. *The Cell-Driven Church.* Kingdom Publishing: Mansfield, Pennsylvania. 2000.

Khong, Lawrence. *The Apostolic Cell Church.* Touch International: Singapore. 2001.

Neighbor, Ralph. *Where Do We Go from Here?* Touch Publications: Houston, Texas. 2000.

Sauder, Brian, and Larry Kreider. *Helping You Build Cell Churches.* DOVE Christian Fellowship International: Ephrata, Pennsylvania. 1998.

Stockstill, Larry. *The Cell Church.* Regal Books: Ventura, California. 1998.

Cell Church Organizations:

Cell Church Solutions: www.cellchurchsolutions.com

Founded by Joel Comiskey offering resources, coaching, and seminars.

TOUCH USA: www.cellgrouppeople.com

Resources and seminars.

Bethany Cell Church Network: www.bccn.org

Closely follows the model of Bogota's International Charismatic Mission. Offers seminars and materials from a "pure G-12" philosophy and a Pentecostal perspective.

Notes

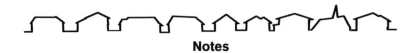

Notes

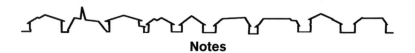

Notes

Notes

Notes

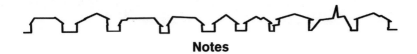

Notes

Notes